MASTER MIND

A True Story of
Obsession, Survival, and Justice

LOU RAGUSE

Post Hill Press

A POST HILL PRESS BOOK
ISBN: 979-8-89565-039-4
ISBN (eBook): 979-8-89565-040-0

Mastermind:
A True Story of Obsession, Survival, and Justice

Cover design by Jim Villaflores

Post Hill Press
New York • Nashville
posthillpress.com

Published in the United States of America
1 2 3 4 5 6 7 8 9 10

Also by the Author

Vanished in Vermillion

CHAPTER ONE

Nicki Lenway glanced at the clock on her dashboard and felt a sudden rush of panic.

Oh, my gosh! I'm going to be late.

The time was 7:28 p.m., and she was sitting in her sport utility vehicle answering a work email on her cell phone. Nicki's job as a forensic scientist for the Minneapolis Police Department included managerial responsibilities, and she was communicating with a fellow supervisor regarding her trainee.

But Nicki was not on duty. She was in the parking lot of FamilyWise, a supervised parenting center on University Avenue in southeast Minneapolis, waiting to pick up her five-year-old son, who was visiting with his father inside. Nicki had been using FamilyWise for several years. First, the center facilitated parental exchanges of her son, Callahan, with her ex-boyfriend, Tim "Atlas" Amacher, without the two parents needing to come face-to-face. Later, they started using the center for supervised visitation.

Their relationship was tumultuous, and their co-parenting experience after breaking up was even worse. Nicki was awarded full custody after a trial, but Atlas continued trying to chip away at her rights by contacting doctors, Child Protection Services, and various police departments. No fewer than ten times over the previous three years, Nicki had to answer and debunk frivolous claims from her ex-boyfriend that she was abusing their son. Eventually, a judge determined Atlas's false reports and repeated trips to urgent care were in and of themselves a form of abuse on Callahan, as the boy was growing more confused by the mixed messages his father was sending him.

Just two months before this cool, rainy April evening, a judge added further restrictions to Atlas's parenting rights by limiting his contact with Callahan to visits at FamilyWise under the supervision of a staff member at the facility. Atlas was humiliated by the fact that he could no longer be alone with his son, and he never wasted an opportunity to blame Nicki to FamilyWise staff as he attempted to charm them and portray the boy's mother as a frivolous instigator driving a wedge between him and his son.

A critical aspect of the supervised parenting center arrangement was that the guidelines prevented Nicki and Atlas from interacting. He was required to arrive at a predetermined time, park in a specified lot, and be in the visitation room when Nicki arrived. She would then park in a separate lot and ring the buzzer at the front door. There would be no way the two would cross paths as a FamilyWise employee would walk Callahan back to Nicki while Atlas remained in the visitation room.

Pickup time was 7:30 p.m., and staff had already scolded Nicki for showing up early toward the end of a prior visit. Since arriving early was discouraged, she and other parents opted to sit in their cars instead of the small waiting room while on-site then ring the buzzer at the front door on time to receive their child from the FamilyWise employee.

At 7:18, Nicki returned to the parking lot after running some errands at Target and HomeGoods—simply burning time during Callahan's visit with Atlas. She was frustrated with herself for letting the next ten minutes slip away. Atlas had conditioned Nicki to constantly worry about being late.

From her interactions with FamilyWise staff, Nicki could tell they had grown to like Atlas—the charismatic and gregarious forty-one-year-old Taekwondo instructor and gym owner. Written reports that the facility eventually turned over to the court during custody proceedings confirmed her suspicions. The FamilyWise notes showed a pattern of compliments toward Atlas and criticism directed at Nicki and her mother, who sometimes picked up Callahan.

It didn't matter that Atlas's lies and reckless behavior had led to the judge ordering the supervised parenting requirement. Atlas had befriended the FamilyWise workers and convinced them that Nicki was the one making things difficult.

Atlas has charmed them into thinking that he's a great dad. If I'm late, it'll just be another thing he tries to use against me, Nicki thought as she began hustling down the sidewalk toward the front door of FamilyWise wearing dark jeans and boots, a long navy blue winter jacket, and a black baseball cap. Years of investigating crime scenes had heightened Nicki's awareness of her surroundings. But not this time. Her mind was on the half-written work email as she anxiously rushed toward the building.

Even the child-swap routine itself was influenced by Nicki's work experiences. In 2019, her coworkers responded to a horrifying crime scene in Minneapolis where a father shot and killed his eight- and eleven-year-old sons as they ran out of their mother's house to greet him. The boys wore backpacks filled with items for their visitation time with their father. The man then went inside the house, stabbed and shot his ex-wife to death, then killed himself.

Like police officers, forensic scientists such as Nicki harden themselves to the emotional aspects of a case to do their jobs properly. However, cases involving children are always difficult. And in that murdered family, Nicki couldn't help but see herself and Callahan. Yes, Atlas seemed to love his son, but hate, anger, and resentment can make people do crazy things. And Nicki's mind was always racing, preparing herself for anything Atlas might try.

On this spring evening, with daylight still lingering, the only scenario on Nicki's mind was how Atlas would portray her as careless and late if she didn't reach the front door in the next few seconds. After taking twenty-four steps from her Nissan Rogue, Nicki sensed someone behind her and turned around.

BANG.

A bullet fired at point-blank range burned through Nicki's neck, puncturing a lung and lodging in her ribs. She fell forward to the ground and rolled onto her back, instinctively crawling away in a crab walk while looking up at a black Sig Sauer .380 caliber handgun pointed at her face.

BANG.

A second bullet traveled straight through Nicki's arm as she raised it in defense.

The shooter was a slender person dressed in black pants and a black, hooded, puffy winter jacket with most of their face covered by a white surgical mask. They circled Nicki, holding the gun with both hands.

BANG.

A third shot, fired in close succession to the other two, somehow missed. Sitting on the ground and desperately pushing herself away, Nicki sprang to her feet when the shooter hesitated, apparently having trouble with the firearm. The shooter began running away, and Nicki lunged toward the front door of FamilyWise. After taking seven strides in the opposite direction, the shooter appeared to clear a jam in the gun and ran toward Nicki again. When the weapon failed to fire what likely would have been the kill shot, the person sprinted away in the same direction from which they came, just eleven seconds after they first pointed the handgun in Nicki's direction.

On her feet and holding her neck with her left hand, Nicki reached the secured FamilyWise entrance, pushed the buzzer/speaker button, and tried asking for help as best she could manage. No response.

Why aren't they letting me in?

An employee inside heard the word "shot" broadcast across the intercom. Instead of unlocking the door, the FamilyWise worker initiated a lockdown procedure they had in place on the chance they needed to protect the children inside from a deranged parent or attacker.

With her son sitting inside the building, expecting her, Nicki momentarily waited for help that wasn't coming. She then dialed 911 herself.

"Nine one one, what is the address of the emergency?" the dispatcher began before Nicki interrupted her with a gurgling sound that Nicki could hardly believe came from her mouth.

Oh my God, I can't speak, Nicki thought as she clutched her neck, applying pressure to both the wound and her vocal cords.

She took a loud, quick gasp for breath as the dispatcher repeated, "What is the address…"

"I've been shot!" Nicki managed to blurt out.

"…of the emergency?" the dispatcher continued.

"Thirty…thirty-six…University," Nicki croaked.

Feeling a sense of suffocation, Nicki loudly breathed in and out several times as the dispatcher once again asked her to verify the address.

Nicki tried again to spell out her location before the dispatcher told her she understood and that an ambulance would be coming. In the meantime, the 911 dispatcher told Nicki to stay on the line.

Still clutching her neck with one hand and her iPhone with the other, Nicki staggered toward a Subaru Outback that had pulled over—the woman driver opening the passenger door.

"Shot!" was all Nicki could articulate.

The woman screamed, "Oh my God! Oh my God! Are you OK?"

Emilie Clancy had been at the stoplight waiting to turn onto University Avenue when she saw the shooter run up to Nicki. After hearing at least two pops, Emilie was so shocked that she waited for the light to turn green at the empty intersection before pulling up next to FamilyWise to help the victim.

As Nicki staggered toward her vehicle, Emilie offered to call 911, but Nicki handed her the phone, already connected.

"Hello, where's the nearest hospital?" Emilie said into the phone, her voice breaking with adrenaline mid-sentence.

The dispatcher assured Emilie that help would arrive soon. While she waited, Emilie grabbed the side of Nicki's neck and pressed down as hard as she could to try and stop the bleeding as Nicki lay in the passenger seat of the parked Subaru.

"We got this. We can do this together," Emilie said to Nicki, looking into her eyes. "Just stay with me. Just keep breathing. Keep looking into my eyes."

Nicki nodded and looked back at Emilie, feeling slight relief from the kindness of the stranger and the promise that the police would come, and she would be taken to the hospital soon. That relief, however, was offset by the fact that her son was still inside FamilyWise, presumably with the one person in the world who wanted Nicki dead.

Atlas had threatened many times that he would disappear with Callahan and that Nicki would never see her son again. Eventually, Nicki began having nightmares where Atlas would carry out that threat, fleeing to Mexico with Callahan and escaping the authorities. As Nicki's mind started to drown in those flooding thoughts, the information Emilie was giving the 911 dispatcher caught her attention.

"The shooter was wearing all black, and he ran right up to her. He was just an arm's length away," Emilie said. "He ran away, but I'm not quite sure which direction he went."

Nicki started shaking her head back and forth. She cleared her throat as best she could and managed one word in a gravelly voice: "Woman." Nicki had no idea who had shot her, but she was sure that the shooter was a woman.

CHAPTER TWO

Nicole Linnette Lenway was born in January 1989—a twin. She and her sister, Chantal Marie Lenway, came home from the hospital to their parents' house in Eden Prairie, Minnesota, where their mother, Rae, would often find them sleeping in the crib holding hands or sucking each other's thumbs.

They are just so connected, Rae constantly thought. She tried moving them into separate cribs when they were three or four months old. Sleeping on opposite sides of the room drove the infants crazy, so Rae had to push the two cribs together.

While the bond between the infant girls was unmistakable, the connection between their twenty-four-year-old mother and her husband, Jody Johnson, was swiftly unraveling. He had lived a hard life, and his issues with jealousy and control were becoming too much for Rae to bear. By the time the twins were eighteen months old, Rae—constantly made to feel unworthy by her husband—left Jody.

Jody allowed Rae to leave the relationship and file for divorce peacefully, and from there, Rae was a twenty-six-year-old single mother who had just weeks earlier returned to her demanding job in sales and service.

If it hadn't been for Donna, her exceptional home daycare provider, Rae doesn't know how she would have gotten through those initial years. There were days Rae would pick the girls up from daycare and head straight back to the office with them. That sometimes meant McDonald's Happy Meal picnics on the office floor as Mom finished her work.

At other times, Donna would care for Nicki and Chantal overnight when Rae traveled for work conferences. The girls played with Donna's three children, who were all close in age and felt like extended family.

For a period after the separation and divorce, Rae still believed the twins' father should be in their lives. She forced the issue to make sure Jody spent time with them. That changed after Rae found out Jody had developed new substance abuse problems since their divorce.

Jody was behind in child support, suffering from chemical abuse and other health issues, and he generally made it clear to Rae that he did not want to take part in any co-parenting. Through mediation, Rae offered to forgive the unpaid child support bill in exchange for sole physical and legal custody of their children. Jody agreed, signed the paperwork, and was out of their lives. The last time he saw the twins was the week before they turned three.

Nicki and her twin sister Chantal.
Photo furnished by Rae Lenway.

Nicki doesn't remember her biological father but can clearly recall when Joe Lenway came into their lives. Rae didn't date much, and when she did, she was reluctant to introduce men to the twins. Protecting them was always her chief concern. However, after seeing Joe several times for lunch dates and other meet-ups that didn't interfere with family time, Joe insisted it was time for him to get to know the girls.

One night, Rae called to cancel an evening date after her babysitter fell through. Instead of calling it off, Joe offered to come to their house, pop popcorn, and watch a movie with the kids. Joe won over Nicki and Chantal with the gesture, showing that he's not above sitting through a Disney princess movie. The comfort he showed in the family setting proved to Rae that Joe would be the rock-solid partner she had longed for.

In September 1995, as the twins began first grade, Joe and Rae got married. Joe gave Nicki and Chantal each a ring with a small diamond as well. They didn't hesitate to start calling him Dad. And Joe wanted to begin the adoption process immediately. After publishing public notices, Joe reached Jody, who agreed to sign the paperwork relinquishing his parental rights. Soon after the girls turned eight, it was official. Everyone in the family was a Lenway.

The Lenway family built a house and moved to Eagan, an eastern suburb of the Twin Cities. Nicki and Chantal became active in competitive soccer, and they also developed a passion for horses.

Rae's sister was a horse trainer, and when the girls were young, the adults took them to a national horse show in Oklahoma. The adults dressed the twins in Western outfits and put them in the lead line class—a competition where the kids simply sat in a saddle, holding on while an instructor walked the horse around the coliseum. Every child participant earned a ribbon and a round of applause, and the rush they felt was enough to hook Nicki and Chantal.

With the help of their aunt, they cared for horses throughout their childhood and teen years, showing them at competitions around the country. They won numerous first-place prizes, and each girl was ranked among the top ten nationally on multiple occasions.

The life lessons the twins picked up in their formative years validated Rae and her sister for fostering that passion. Nicki and Chantal learned to feed and groom the animals at their aunt's stable. They bathed them, cleaned the stalls, and cared for the horses when they were sick. Rae could see how much the experience taught the girls about dedication, perseverance, hard work, and discipline. Along the way, the twins each developed a great deal of empathy.

While Rae never tested to confirm if Nicki and Chantal were identical twins, the two looked a lot alike. As kids, Nicki enjoyed pranking teachers and classmates by switching spots with her sister—up until the moment she would learn Chantal had a test or major assignment due.

As a child, Nicki was the more extroverted and vivacious of the two. So much so that while grocery shopping, Rae would find her in the next aisle chattering away with another shopper despite warnings not to talk to strangers. At the same time, Chantal would hide behind her mom's legs if someone asked her a question. At home, Chantal refused to leave her sister's side, holding Nicki's hand in the corner of the living room when Rae sent the more mischievous girl into time-out.

When the girls reached their teens, Rae noticed that some of their characteristics swapped. Chantal became the social butterfly, and Rae literally needed to force Nicki out of her textbooks on a Friday night to go out with her friends. All the while, Nicki and Chantal maintained their quintessential twin-sibling relationship, working together at a retail store in the Mall of America, getting a kick out of customers who would double-take upon noticing their striking resemblance.

The Lenway family. Photo furnished by Rae Lenway.

From a young age, Nicki thought it would be fun to one day become a police officer. She loved watching shows like *CSI: Crime Scene Investigation*, one of the most popular prime-time dramas on network TV.

During her senior year of high school, Nicki took a forensic science course that helped narrow her career focus. Rather than conducting interrogations and making arrests as a sworn officer, she saw a future as a forensic scientist—a crime scene investigator specializing in lifting fingerprints and swabbing for DNA, the intricate work that helps solve complex criminal investigations through evidence collection and analysis.

Nicki had received a scholarship offer from the University of Puget Sound in Tacoma, Washington, but her high school forensic science class revealed a calling she wanted to follow. She changed her plans and instead applied to Hamline University in Saint Paul, Minnesota, which offered a forensic science program. She majored in biology and criminal justice and earned a post-baccalaureate certificate in forensic science.

Chantal also decided to attend college close to home, at the University of St. Thomas in Saint Paul. She majored in psychology and aimed to become a children's play therapist. After spending their freshman year in the dorms, the twins and Nicki's friend, Anya Esch, lived together in a house for the rest of their college years.

The three young women had their professional lives in front of them. While Anya was engaged to marry her high school sweetheart, Nicki was single and open to meeting people. Anya had started working out at a gym in White Bear Lake, and she invited Nicki to join her. That's where Nicki would meet the man who would change the course of her life.

CHAPTER THREE

A group of a dozen sweaty men and women lined up on the red and black Taekwondo mat, resembling soldiers in boot camp. Their instructor, Atlas—a muscular Black man with a shaved head, wearing black Adidas workout pants and a black ribbed tank top—cranked up the volume on the studio's sound system. Amid the synth build-up and blaring lyrics from Pitbull's top hit, Atlas cracked a joke at the expense of one of his best friends taking part in the class.

"C'mon, Aaron, ten more!" Atlas shouted at the man who was bear-crawling across the mat. "You gotta work off all those Fourth of July beers!"

The entire class, a tight-knit community, laughed as they strained through another set of bear crawls to open the workout led by the magnetic fitness instructor. The year was 2012, and the class was called XFT—Extreme Fitness Training—a blend of CrossFit and boot camp fitness, which drew a dedicated following based on word of mouth. Half of the students in the class didn't even know the thirty-one-year-old gym owner's real name. Timothy Allen Amacher was given the nickname Atlas, from the Greek mythology figure who holds the world on his shoulders, by his breakdancing teammates ten years earlier. Tim insisted that everyone, aside from his Taekwondo students and families, call him Atlas.

Atlas was part-owner and lead instructor of World Taekwondo Academy in White Bear Lake. His students and their families called him Master Amacher inside and outside of the class setting. "Master" was a title he earned through years of training and mastery of the martial art of Taekwondo. Running the Taekwondo studio was his full-time job, but Atlas also conducted personal training sessions in the studio's basement weight room known as Underground Gym. While teaching XFT, his trademark fitness class, Atlas utilized the entire building inside and out. XFT is what Atlas built his social life around after reaching his thirties. After class on Tuesday and Thursday evenings, the group would go out for drinks together at the Blue Door Pub. After class on Saturday mornings, the group would go out for brunch.

As Nicki's friend Anya reached the best shape of her life leading up to her wedding, Nicki finally agreed to join her at the gym owned by the man with infectious energy. The first day the attractive twenty-three-year-old arrived, fellow trainer John Swoboda noticed Atlas's gaze follow the thin blonde as she walked across the studio. John shook his head, knowing just what Atlas was thinking. He always laid claim to training the most beautiful women who joined Underground Gym. As soon as he met Nicki—smitten the moment he looked into her piercing blue/grey eyes—Atlas laid it on thick, leaving no question that he was pursuing her.

At first, Nicki was put off by Atlas's pushiness. As the weeks passed, she began bonding with others in the class and enjoying the get togethers afterward, growing a sense of community with her fellow XFT members. Nicki was starting to tire of turning down Atlas each time he wanted to do something outside the group setting. Finally, she relented.

"OK, if you stop bothering me, I'll go on one date with you," Nicki coyly answered him. "And after that, I don't want to hear it."

To her surprise, Nicki had a blast on that first date. They spent the day making stops at different bars on Atlas's motorcycle. They went dancing. And she learned more about the man who always seemed to be the center of attention everywhere he went.

Timothy Allen Amacher was born in March 1981 in Saint Paul, Minnesota, where he grew up and spent most of his life. His parents passed down a diverse heritage—African American, Puerto Rican, and German—but he identifies as Black.

A defining moment of Tim's childhood was when his father, Mark, killed himself at age thirty-seven. Tim was eleven. The resulting trauma sometimes led to self-destructive behavior throughout Tim's childhood and adult life, as well as Tim's belief that he, too, might someday die young. In the immediate years after his father's death, Tim picked fights, didn't listen to authority, and altogether didn't care what happened to himself. He told people that Taekwondo changed that.

Grandmaster Byung Yul Lee ran World Taekwondo Academy in Saint Paul after emigrating from Korea to the United States. After young Tim walked into his studio, Grandmaster Lee took the boy under his wing. Taking on a role as his mentor, Grandmaster Lee served as a father figure to Tim, teaching him respect and discipline.

"And when you become a better person, you're better for your community, better for those around you," Tim told White Bear Lake Magazine in 2014 for a profile they wrote on how he was carrying on his mentor's legacy.

When Tim was in his early twenties, the persona of "Atlas" was born. He led a small group of hip-hop breakdancers called the Groove Nutz Crew. They were consistently one of the top groups in Minnesota in the 2000s with moves that seemed to defy gravity. Groove Nutz even performed with some significant up-and-coming hip-hop artists as backup dancers.

In 2006, Atlas began to phase out his breakdancing career when he returned to Taekwondo. He became an instructor at Grandmaster Lee's studio before eventually taking over and moving the business to White Bear Lake. There, the persona of Master Amacher was born, positively influencing the lives of scores of children over the years. Many of those kids came into Master Amacher's studio during a very rough period in their lives, just as he had when he met his mentor at the age of twelve. Each year, World Taekwondo Academy hosted a day camp for kids during summer vacation. Master Amacher led classes and excursions for the children in the popular program, cementing with their parents a reputation as a trusted leader.

Master Amacher instructs a Taekwondo student.

Nicki could tell Atlas's past trauma still affected him deeply as an adult, but as a pair, it didn't take long for them to mesh. Atlas was extroverted, Nicki was introverted, and their social lives together were a lot of fun. They'd go out in groups, including Anya, her husband, and other friends from Underground Gym. They embraced the nightlife, including bottle service at clubs in downtown Minneapolis. Before long, Atlas and Nicki were in an exclusive relationship.

While Nicki sensed Atlas likely had an extensive dating history, she had no idea what some of his guy friends had seen. In his early twenties, Atlas's mother sold him her duplex in Saint Paul, Minnesota, making him a very young homeowner. His next-door neighbor, Charlie Dettloff, noticed Atlas installed a purple porch light above his front door. Charlie asked about it, and Atlas explained that when the light was on, it meant he was "open for business." When the light was off, women in Atlas's life who drove past knew he was with someone inside. While it sounded unbelievable, Charlie started to notice women parking cars outside the home and waiting to enter when the purple light turned on.

After Atlas stopped performing with his breakdancing crew, he continued dancing for fun at clubs in Minneapolis on weekends. With his friend Aaron Howell, they would cockily strut onto the middle of the dance floor and start moving, and everyone else would clear out—all eyes on them. The attention was intoxicating, and Aaron remembered literally having to run from women at those clubs who wanted a piece of Atlas. Their weekend club-hopping lasted nearly until the timeframe that Atlas met Nicki.

After Atlas and Nicki started dating, Anya noticed some red flags at the studio and gym when Nicki wasn't there. Atlas continued to flirt with other women who came in for personal training. Rumors about affairs with other clients and even married mothers of Taekwondo students always seemed to hover around Atlas. Everyone who knew him well wondered whether he still presented himself as "open for business" behind Nicki's back.

It was undeniable, however, that Nicki and Atlas were having fun, and their relationship was progressing. When Nicki met Dimitris Kelly, one of Atlas's best friends, Dimitris quizzed her on Atlas's real name.

"Tim," she correctly answered.

"Oh, so he actually likes you," Dimitris teased.

Nicki and Atlas. Photo furnished by Rae Lenway.

With her personal life flourishing in 2012, Nicki received great news on the professional front. She had gotten her dream job. The City of Minneapolis hired her to be a forensic scientist. That meant grueling hours, as she would have to work night shifts for the foreseeable future, but the accomplishment marked the culmination of years of studying and hard work.

Atlas was initially proud and supportive. He was dating a real-life crime scene investigator who looked like she could be an actress on the TV show *CSI*. Atlas bragged to his friends who worked in the Saint Paul Police Department about Nicki's new job across the Mississippi River in Minneapolis. While everything at that time felt right, Nicki would soon learn that Atlas's support would vaporize when she needed it most.

CHAPTER FOUR

One night in June 2013, Nicki was riding along with two officers from the Fourth Precinct of the Minneapolis Police Department as part of the training program for Nicki's new role. As Nicki and the officers got to know each other, she told them about her twin sister Chantal, who worked at a nearby neighborhood hangout in Northeast Minneapolis, The 1029 Bar. It was a place regulars described as a "*Cheers* bar" because—like the TV show—the workers and customers were so familiar with each other.

"Let's stop in and say hi!" the officers suggested since their shift had slowed down just before 10:00 p.m., and they weren't on any active calls.

Nicki called her sister to let her know they'd be swinging by, but Chantal told her she'd called in sick and was home at their parents' house. Chantal suffered from an affliction called cyclic vomiting syndrome (CVS), known among sufferers as "abdominal migraines," which consisted of cycles of nausea brought on by stress.

"I'm just going to have a low-key night and take a bath," Chantal told her sister.

"OK, I hope you feel better. I love you. I'll see you soon," Nicki said.

The next day, Nicki was working at Caribou Coffee, where she still picked up occasional shifts while completing her training at her full-time job. Early in the shift, Rae called Nicki and asked if she'd heard from her sister. Rae didn't see Chantal at home before she went to work. In the afternoon, a friend reached out to Rae to let her know Chantal had missed a lunch date—something that was unlike her.

"I wouldn't be too concerned; she's probably resting," Nicki told her mom, filling her in on what Chantal had told her the night before. The Lenways were all very aware of how debilitating Chan's CVS could be at times.

A little later into her shift, however, Nicki received a cryptic call from her mom, telling her that she needed to come straight home due to a family emergency and that a family friend would pick her up, so she wouldn't have to drive. Rae did not tell her in that call that a neighbor she had asked to check on Chantal made a horrible discovery.

Nicki later wondered how she didn't put the pieces together herself. When the family friend arrived to pick her up, Nicki assumed the emergency must involve her elderly great-grandmother.

"What's going on? My mom won't tell me," Nicki pleaded with Scott during the half-hour ride back to her parents' home.

"It's your sister. She's gone," Scott gingerly revealed. "I'm sorry, kiddo, I really don't know much else."

The rest of the ride was very quiet as Nicki went into shock. Nicki's twin sister, who had always felt like an extended part of her, had died in their parents' home at age twenty-four.

The rest of the day and those that followed felt surreal. Aside from the CVS, Chantal was very healthy and had played competitive soccer her whole life. A medical examiner searched for answers, finding that Chantal had a heart defect and died when her heart simply stopped beating. The Lenways examined Chan's phone and saw that Nicki was the last to communicate with her.

"I love you. I'll see you soon," were Nicki's last words to her sister.

As Nicki's grief reduced her to a shell of herself, her friend Anya offered the support she needed. Anya stayed with the Lenways for several days and continued helping Nicki for several months afterward. She contacted Nicki's boss at the Minneapolis Police Department Crime Lab. Even though Nicki hadn't accrued any sick or vacation time yet, her new coworkers donated their paid time off to Nicki, so she could stay home as long as she needed. Anya even tried motivating Atlas to step up and be the partner Nicki needed him to be as she went through the toughest time of her life.

Atlas was uncomfortable and wanted to remain hands-off. He made only a brief appearance at Chantal's wake. For the funeral, the Lenways asked everyone to wear a flash of pink, Chan's favorite color. Atlas seemed bothered by that simple request, leading Nicki to believe he wouldn't come to the funeral because he didn't want to wear the pink button-up dress shirt she purchased for him.

"I shouldn't have to talk you into this," Nicki told him. "If you're not going to go, you're not going to go."

He ended up attending the funeral, then leaving immediately afterward, returning to his gym, where he truly felt at home.

Nicki's family and friends were far from impressed by her boyfriend during the days and weeks following Chantal's death. They didn't realize, however, that Atlas had already begun to condition Nicki under his control by that point in their relationship.

If Nicki were ever at a family gathering or friend event without him, Atlas would relentlessly call or text Nicki until she eventually answered. When she finally did, he would pick fights and make her feel so anxious and uncomfortable that she no longer wanted to be at the event. In that backward way, Nicki then felt relief when she left her family or friend situation and returned to him.

That situation played out in front of Rae and Joe about a week after the funeral when the family was cleaning out Chantal's car together. Atlas called Nicki's phone several times until she answered it. Then she began answering his calls, talking for a moment or two, letting him know what they were doing, then hanging up. Atlas continued calling back—up to twelve times within half an hour—until Joe lost it and answered Nicki's phone himself.

"Stop calling! We're busy!" Joe yelled, perplexed by the lack of empathy Atlas was showing their family.

Throughout their young adult lives, Chantal had always brought out Nicki's outgoing and social side. After Chan's death, her twin became more introverted and guarded. Had the tragedy not occurred, Nicki and Atlas might have broken up around that time since they were drifting apart in many ways. However, grief can have unpredictable effects on people. Overwhelmed by her sense of loss, Nicki couldn't imagine having to cope with losing anyone else in her life at that moment.

Nicki's bosses were extremely empathetic when she returned to her job, not wanting to push her comfort levels as they prepared her to work in sometimes gruesome crime scenes. They knew they had a star in the making, and she soon began impressing them with her crime scene processing skills. Coworkers, friends, and family members gave Nicki the support to start moving forward after the death of her sister. That support may have made it easier to overlook what was missing with Atlas, and the couple moved forward in their relationship as well.

CHAPTER FIVE

On Halloween weekend 2013, Nicki wanted to get out and have fun. Leaving the house socially had taken a lot of effort in the four months since Chantal's death. Nicki and Atlas rented a hotel room at the Westin in downtown Minneapolis and dressed in costume as Kitana and Raiden from the *Mortal Kombat* video games and movies. They planned a night of fun with Nicki's cousin, Crystal, and her longtime boyfriend, Joe, along with some of Atlas's friends. They met at First Avenue, the iconic Minneapolis bar and music venue made famous by Prince.

As the night progressed, everyone in the group drank plenty of alcohol, especially Atlas. Crystal excused herself from the group to use the bathroom at one point, and Atlas slipped away to follow her. Once he thought they were out of Nicki and Joe's sight, Atlas made his move on Crystal. He tugged on her arm from behind, and when Crystal spun around, Atlas pushed her against the wall and tried to kiss her. Crystal resisted, and

Atlas tried pulling her into the men's bathroom, grabbing her by the butt.

Shocked at Atlas's brazen and inappropriate actions, Crystal braced herself to prevent Atlas from pulling her further. They were interrupted by Crystal's boyfriend, who instinctively followed Atlas when he left the table.

"What's going on?" Joe shouted, creating separation between them.

Seeing that Joe knew the truth, Crystal ran to Nicki to inform her of what Atlas had just attempted.

"Atlas just tried kissing me and pulling me into the restroom with him. We should leave, and you should come with us," Crystal told Nicki.

Atlas arrived at their side seconds later, loudly contradicting Crystal's story.

"She's lying! Crystal's drunk. She's doing this. She's the one who came onto me," Atlas told Nicki as he attempted to sound sober, anger piercing through in his tone.

Earlier in the evening, before meeting up with her cousin, Nicki mentioned to Atlas that Crystal used to get pretty wild when they would party together in college. Atlas began utilizing that information to support his lies about Crystal.

"Your *own cousin* is trying to come onto me, Lenway," Atlas said, his voice rising. "She's a drama queen. She is acting like a whore!"

"You're coming home with us," Crystal repeated to Nicki.

As Atlas and Crystal began screaming at each other, Nicki tried wrapping her head around the accusations both were making. Being very conflict-averse, the screaming upset Nicki as much as the content of the argument, so she pulled Atlas outside the noisy nightclub to continue talking on the sidewalk out front. She didn't want to doubt her own cousin, but Nicki knew Crystal had been drinking heavily.

An eerily similar scenario played out months earlier when Atlas accused one of Nicki's acquaintances of making romantic moves on him. In that instance, Atlas pulled Nicki aside and claimed the woman asked him, "Why would you be with her when you could be with someone like me?" Hearing that angered Nicki. She confronted that woman and argued at the bar before leaving with the issue unresolved. Nicki believed Atlas over her acquaintance in that odd dispute, but now she was doubting herself and Atlas.

As Nicki started to question Atlas's version of the story this time, he shut her down each time she spoke, aghast that Nicki would believe her cousin's word over his. Curse words began flowing out of his mouth as he publicly berated her. Nicki started getting confused—feeling conflicted and forced into the role of peacemaker as Atlas belittled Nicki and her cousin.

"You are being so fucking irrational," Atlas shouted as Nicki began crying.

Crystal and Joe attempted to step between them.

"I saw exactly what happened," Joe said, trying to show Nicki that Atlas was gaslighting her within this tumultuous argument.

Atlas took a defensive posture toward Joe and Crystal as if their intervention was about to turn violent. He screamed at the couple to back up and leave them alone.

"Crystal's making it up," Atlas yelled in Nicki's face. "She's doing this because she doesn't like me."

The scene Atlas was making outside First Avenue started drawing the attention of other costumed partiers. Nicki wanted to diffuse the tension and didn't want to choose sides between her boyfriend and her cousin. She started walking back to the Westin, upset, with Atlas following behind.

Crystal, however, was deeply disturbed by what had just happened. She continued texting Nicki that night.

"I don't want you to be with him tonight," Crystal wrote. "I'm worried for your safety. If he's doing this to your cousin, what does that say? I'm being honest. He's lying to you. Joe saw it all. You can talk to Joe."

Crystal's concerns lingered through the weekend, and on Monday morning, she called Nicki's mom to tell her the story. Rae was close with her niece, but it was unusual for Crystal to call her under such circumstances.

"I want to tell you about something, but I'm really hesitant to tell you because you're going to freak out," Crystal told her aunt before recounting the disturbing events of their Halloween night in dramatic fashion.

Rae wondered if it was possible Crystal misread something from Atlas. Would he really hit on Nicki's cousin in public? That just didn't make any rational sense. But Rae called Crystal's boyfriend Joe, who confirmed that he witnessed things play out precisely as Crystal described.

Later that night, Rae reached Nicki, understandably concerned.

"I don't know really what happened, but I'm concerned," Rae said. "Crystal is worried for your safety."

"No, it's fine. Crystal shouldn't have exploded like that," Nicki tried to assure her mom. "You know how Crystal can sensationalize things."

"You need to talk to Atlas," Rae responded. "This is not OK. You need to have a conversation with him."

Rae and her husband Joe had previously been alarmed by Atlas's behavior after Chantal's death and now were starting to feel disturbed by the kind of man their daughter was dating. Still, just as most young adults would react, Nicki didn't give her parents a full picture of her troubles with Atlas. She knew they would have a difficult time getting past the negative aspects of her partner in order to see what she saw in him.

Like with every fight, big or small, when Nicki attempted to revisit and address the issue with Atlas, he took control of the conversation with his strategy of denying, deflecting, and blaming. It never took long before Nicki felt verbally beaten into submission, and the issue became too challenging to address further.

After the excitement surrounding the start of what seems to be a promising relationship, it can be challenging for a victim demoralized by intimidation, control, and manipulation to recognize those behaviors as their partner's "true self." Nicki found herself constantly searching for the good person she had met at the Taekwondo studio and quickly fell in love with. By the time more serious red flags with Atlas emerged, Nicki had moved in with him at his Saint Paul duplex. That made the prospect of ending the relationship quite daunting, especially when Atlas continued to show Nicki glimpses of the man she had fallen for. Atlas would frequently reassure Nicki that he was working on himself all while twisting reality just enough to make her question whether she was the one to blame for the faults and flaws in their relationship.

The Halloween episode at First Avenue was one of the few times Atlas let his anger boil over in front of friends. He would usually bottle up those feelings and maintain his calm, charismatic demeanor while out with others. When he got home, and the front door shut, he would then typically begin dressing down Nicki for "humiliating" him.

About a year later, on a cold winter night, Atlas's good friends witnessed another explosive event between the couple. They were sitting around a familiar table at The 1029 Bar in Northeast Minneapolis, where Chantal had worked with her good friend Alayna. The day Chan missed her lunch date, it was Alayna who alerted Rae that she hadn't shown up and knew something was wrong. Since that day, Alayna felt a strong duty to protect and care for her late friend's family.

On that chilly evening at The 1029, Nicki was enjoying a light conversation with Atlas and his friends. Alayna was on shift behind the bar, watching Atlas's temper quickly heat up as Nicki's phone buzzed. Nicki casually glanced at it and saw a text message from a college ex-boyfriend. The man had since moved out of state, but he and Nicki remained friends and occasionally checked in on each other via text. The message was unsolicited, and the content was innocuous. Still, Nicki knew it was precisely the kind of thing that could set Atlas off in a jealous rage. She nonchalantly put the phone back on the table, screen-side down, but Atlas noticed.

"Who was that?" he asked in front of the group.

"Nobody. It's no big deal," Nicki responded.

"Why are you being secretive about it?" Atlas asked, his tone growing more accusatory.

As the tension rose, Atlas grabbed the phone away from Nicki, read the text, and began to lose it in front of his friends.

"What are you doing texting with your ex? Are you cheating on me? This is why I can't trust you," Atlas started shouting at Nicki at the table.

The others tried to tell Atlas to "chill out" and that he and Nicki could discuss the issue when they got home. Nicki tried to defend herself.

"I didn't do anything! I'm not texting back," she said.

"You're lying to me, you whore!" Atlas hissed back, which sent Nicki running to the bathroom crying.

Alayna, who witnessed the entire event unfold from behind the bar, followed her. Although Alayna didn't know precisely what Atlas was arguing about, she helped her friend regain her composure until Nicki convinced her to return to work.

Moments later, Alayna noticed that Nicki and Atlas were no longer at the table. She grabbed Nicki's coat and found the couple outside in the cold, Atlas yelling at her while holding Nicki's arms in place, so she couldn't leave.

"Are you OK, Nicki? I have your coat," Alayna said.

"We are fine," Atlas answered for her.

"She doesn't look fine," Alayna responded.

"I don't even know you, Pinkie; leave us alone," Atlas said, referring to Alayna's pink shirt.

Alayna reminded Atlas that they had met at least two other times and said she would only leave if Nicki asked her to. Nicki—cold, wet, and distraught—tried to assure Alayna she would be OK.

"I'm so sorry. I didn't mean to bring this drama here," Nicki said.

"You are not in trouble. You are not the one doing anything wrong," Alayna responded.

Nicki was getting used to apologizing for Atlas's behavior when he caused a scene because he conditioned her to believe it was her fault—that she brought it out of him.

After leaving Nicki's side, Alayna asked The 1029 Bar bouncer to keep an eye on Atlas, warning him that she was worried about Nicki's safety. The bouncer, Big B, didn't waste much time approaching Atlas.

"You need to leave. You can't be doing that here," Big B said.

Atlas turned to Nicki and said, "If you weren't so emotional and causing such a scene, Lenway, we wouldn't be kicked out right now."

Nicki wasn't the one getting kicked out, but she left with Atlas, feeling guilty again for what had transpired in front of friends and acquaintances.

Alayna was so disturbed by the incident that—like Nicki's cousin Crystal—she too called Rae the next day to describe the verbal and emotional abuse she witnessed. Alayna considered Nicki, her parents, and her late sister Chantal some of the kindest and most compassionate people she had ever met, and she was shaken by the thought of what Nicki's relationship must be like behind closed doors.

The phone call felt like déjà vu for Rae. She and her husband, Joe, began thinking back on some of the other red flags they had witnessed over the nearly two-year relationship. Early on, before Chantal's death, Rae was eating with Nicki, Atlas, and some of their friends at The 1029 Bar. After a few drinks, Atlas began boastfully telling stories to the playful groans of the group. To Rae, he teasingly said, "Oh, come on, you know that you love me."

"Oh, I don't know. The jury's still out!" Rae ribbed back.

Atlas didn't think the joke was funny.

"What?!" he responded.

"Come on, you still have to prove yourself," Rae teased.

Atlas began sulking, looking in the other direction, and refusing to acknowledge Rae at the table for the rest of their dinner. Atlas's fragile ego stuck out, but Rae blew it off at the time, not wanting to make early judgments about him.

After Nicki and Atlas had been dating for more than a year, the Lenways were together at a wedding for one of Nicki's childhood friends. Nicki, Atlas, Rae, and Joe—along with two other couples—were seated together at the same table for the reception. Soon enough, as is often the case at weddings, the table small talk shifted to the topic of "growing old together," and someone asked Nicki and Atlas about their future plans. In private, Atlas would talk about one day getting married. However, Atlas quickly shut it down in front of Nicki's parents.

"Yeah, I don't make commitments like that," Atlas said.

"What do you mean?" Rae asked.

"I'm going to die by the time I'm forty anyway," Atlas said.

"Excuse me?" Rae asked.

"You know what they say, die young and leave a good-looking corpse," Atlas laughed.

He made the comment jokingly, adding that his father died young, and he had accepted the fact he was on the same path. No one else at the table was laughing. Although Nicki appeared unfazed, Rae was deeply offended and did not keep her feelings to herself.

"That is not funny at all. You're in a serious relationship with our daughter, and you're saying you're going to die young and not be here for her? That's not OK," Rae said.

"Well, it's going to happen anyway. I don't have a good family history," Atlas reiterated, again laughing away the comments and moving the conversation topic away from his bad "joke."

Joke or not, Nicki's parents and friends didn't realize the extent to which Atlas would use his father's suicide as an excuse for his actions and the extent to which he would use the threat of suicide to keep Nicki from ending their relationship over the months to come.

CHAPTER SIX

Nicki and Atlas's relationship continued into 2015 but was rocky for much of the year. In July, the couple took a trip to Las Vegas with some of Atlas's buddies. From the beginning, the trip seemed doomed. Everything appeared fine in a group setting, but they started arguing as soon as the two were alone. At one point, Atlas accused Nicki of flirting with one of the other guys on the trip. And then, things escalated while they were out for dinner on the last night of the vacation.

From Nicki's perspective, the experience at the restaurant started out refreshing because the couple was getting along for the first time. That quickly changed after Nicki—who admits she sometimes has "OCD tendencies" about cleanliness—scooped up some crumbs from their table and put them on another plate. Atlas, extremely annoyed, flipped a switch and began icing Nicki out. He dramatically threw down his napkin, paid their bill in a huff, and started walking out of the restaurant ahead of his girlfriend.

Nicki hadn't pieced together what had angered Atlas yet, and she started demanding to know what was wrong.

"What's going on? Why are you upset? What's happening? I can tell you're upset," she said.

Nicki's questions only bothered Atlas more. He walked very briskly down the Vegas Strip. Nicki started getting lost in the crowd behind him, and she was forced to run to catch up to him. They reached the Flamingo Hotel, where they were staying, and entered the elevator together.

"What is going on? What's wrong? What did I do this time?" Nicki continued.

"Stop talking!" Atlas screamed as he kicked the elevator door with all his strength, leaving a dent.

Once inside their hotel room, Atlas picked up a lamp and threw it.

"You ruined the trip, Lenway!" he screamed.

Nicki locked herself in the bathroom as Atlas's tirade continued. Atlas kept screaming nonsense, banging on the door, and chugging from a large bottle of vodka in the room.

Nicki called her mom, revealing in real-time how much Atlas could scare her. Rae encouraged her to call security, but Nicki didn't want to cause a scene. She assured her mom she would sleep in the bathtub and that things would be fine after Atlas passed out.

They had an early morning flight back to Minnesota, so Nicki needed to wake Atlas up hours later, still drunk. After making it to their airport gate, Atlas began puking, and the crew had to hold the flight for several minutes before he could board.

The trip was a disaster, but it did not spell the immediate end of the relationship. Like most of Atlas's repetitive, explosive tirades, this one was fueled by alcohol. As he had done many times before, Atlas swore that he would quit drinking.

He would go through stretches without touching alcohol, then periods where all he did was drink to excess. There was no in-between. Atlas reminded Nicki that he was going to therapy and promised to continue. He insisted he was making progress.

"He's sober now. We're good. Everything's fine. I'm safe," Nicki texted her mom once things settled down on the way home from Vegas.

Atlas would blame his anger and outbursts on how his childhood shaped him. He claimed he was abused while growing up. His parents divorced, and Atlas's mother was extremely hard on his father. He'd say that made relationships difficult for him. "Trust is hard." By shifting the burden onto Nicki, she would find herself at fault for not being a better, more understanding partner for Atlas. She would parrot those same excuses to friends and family when explaining his behavior and justifying staying with him.

"I know I have these issues. I'm working on it. I promise I'll be better. I'll change," Atlas would typically say after an exhausting argument or scary incident like the Vegas trip. The empath in Nicki wanted to see the best in Atlas. She looked past the empty promises, convincing herself that his worst moments were merely the cost of loving someone who'd been broken long before she met him.

That sucks; everyone who grows up like that or has to deal with those kinds of things is going to be messed up to a certain degree, she thought.

And, of course, there was Atlas's father's suicide. He warned Nicki that if she left him, he might end up just like his dad. Atlas viewed suicide as inevitable, a fate he felt powerless to escape—unless she stayed. Unless she saved him.

One night that fall, Atlas woke Nicki up at 2:00 a.m. and started an argument in the bedroom of their Saint Paul home—a routine that had played out countless times before. As Nicki groggily began responding, Atlas said, "You need to get out. You need to leave," as he would always say at the peak of their arguments at home.

Usually when that scene took place, Nicki would respond, "It's two in the morning. Where am I supposed to go? I live here."

However, Nicki had decided this particular fight would be the last of its sort. "Fine, I'll leave. I don't care," she responded. Nicki packed an overnight bag in the bedroom and started walking toward the front door. She planned to leave the house, get to her car, and just figure out what to do next.

Nicki made it as far as the stairway at the duplex entrance when she felt her head jerk back. Atlas had grabbed hold of Nicki's ponytail and started pulling her back inside as she fell to the floor.

"You're not leaving," Atlas growled as Nicki flailed her arms, trying to break Atlas's grip as he dragged her by the hair across the stairs and into the living room, the front door of the duplex closing behind them.

Once free, Nicki ran into the guest bedroom and locked the door behind her, which she had done many times during fights when Atlas's anger rose, and she felt unsafe. Despite the fear he often caused her, physical abuse to this degree hadn't happened before. Earlier in the relationship, Atlas once slapped Nicki across the face with an open hand. During fights, he often pinned her against the wall or held her in place with his hands on her upper arms. Atlas would regularly use his size to intimidate. Although his verbal and emotional abuse was commonplace throughout their nearly three-year relationship, being dragged across the floor by her ponytail was the most scared Nicki had been for her physical safety.

"If you leave tonight, I'm changing the locks, and you'll never be able to get back in to get your stuff," Atlas warned her.

"I'm good. Everything's good," Nicki responded through the bedroom door to pacify him. To Nicki, though, nothing was good. She needed separation from Atlas for her physical and psychological well-being.

The next morning, Nicki called her mom.

"I can't take it anymore," Nicki said, giving Rae a little more insight into the control she'd been enduring in her relationship but leaving out the details of the physical violence. Nicki did not want to move back in with her parents. Besides having decided after college that she was too independent to live at home as an adult, Nicki didn't want to immediately pack up and leave Atlas's house. She was afraid of how he might react and retaliate if she enacted a hard break-up that day. Nicki asked her mom if she would help her begin looking for a home of her own.

Rae and Joe agreed to help Nicki financially with a down payment on her own house. At first, Atlas protested Nicki's house hunting, telling her they should buy a property together instead. But Nicki's plan to gingerly withdraw from the relationship seemed to be working, as she thought Atlas finally could see that things between them were no longer the same.

After closing on a house in Northeast Minneapolis, Nicki felt ready to move on with life. Her career at the Minneapolis Police Department was taking off. She was making more money and finally had more freedom. Less than two months after that horrifying ponytail-dragging incident, however, a shocking twist made Nicki realize that Tim Amacher might never be out of her life.

CHAPTER SEVEN

Working overnight shifts is challenging in any profession. Some people simply can't handle how their bodies react to the upside-down schedule and the taxing effects that conforming the rest of their lives to societal norms has on them. Fortunately, Nicki managed to cope well for the first three years of her job, collecting evidence at crime scenes while the rest of the city slept. However, in November 2015, she began to struggle. As she prepared to leave work sick with nausea for the third consecutive night, a coworker joked, "I bet you're pregnant."

That prompted Nicki to take a test. And sure enough, it was positive. That result didn't make sense. Nicki was on birth control and recently had her period. She immediately contacted Atlas to let him know, and his reaction was initially supportive.

"It's OK, we'll figure it out," he said.

That support did not last long, however, as Atlas began wavering during those first two weeks between claiming someone else must be the father—something that was an impossibility—and a paranoid theory accusing Nicki of intentionally skipping her birth control pill in order to "trap him." That didn't make sense either as they were split up and were living in separate houses. Atlas then began pressuring Nicki to abort the pregnancy.

"We didn't plan this. You should get rid of it. We're not in a good spot," Atlas said, suggesting that he and Nicki repair their nonexistent relationship, then try for a baby when "the timing is better."

"We should get married, and then down the line, we'll have kids," Atlas said.

Atlas had not given up hope of rekindling things with Nicki after she moved out. Nicki hadn't given him a hard no, either. She was walking a fine line and trying not to upset him. While she didn't completely close the door on the possibility of reconciliation, Nicki was firm regarding the pregnancy and her choice to have the baby.

"It's my decision," Nicki told Atlas. "If you don't want to be involved, don't be involved. I'm perfectly capable of having a child with or without you. You can choose whether you want to be a part of this or not, but I'm having this baby."

After about two weeks, Nicki made the difficult call to her mom. She drove to her parents' house and shared all of her fears and apprehensions—along with her commitment to having and raising the baby herself. She was old enough, mature enough, and had a stable job and lots of support around her. And for better or worse, Atlas had made it abundantly clear he wanted nothing to do with it. Still, Nicki couldn't help but feel embarrassed.

"This isn't how I planned my life to go," Nicki cried.

Rae assured Nicki that she and Joe supported her no matter what. They never expressed any disappointment or anything less than kindness to their daughter.

"Whatever you need from us, we'll figure this out," Rae said. "You're fully capable."

Rae accompanied Nicki to all the doctor's appointments, as Atlas chose to stay away. When Nicki received her first ultrasound to determine the age of the fetus, she learned she would be giving birth to a baby boy with an expected due date of June 9, 2016.

At times throughout the pregnancy, Nicki was hopeful that Atlas would come around, so they could look forward to a manageable co-parenting arrangement. She saw how good he was with kids at World Taekwondo Academy, where dozens of boys and girls looked up to Master Amacher as a role model. Atlas loved kids. He wasn't faking that. Nicki's swirling emotions and fears about raising a child alone also led to her feeling open to getting back together with Atlas.

Maybe this is what it will take for him to grow up and figure it out, to stop being the way he is, Nicki hoped.

They met for dinners and other casual dates during the pregnancy. Atlas's efforts varied depending on the week. He would try to convince Nicki that they should get married to raise their child in a two-parent household, and then he would continue his resentment toward Nicki for her decision to have the baby. When he'd raise her already settled decision during an argument, he'd find ways to accuse her of choosing the baby over him since that's not what he wanted.

Atlas didn't tell any of his friends or clients at the gym that he was going to have a child, which created a lot of awkwardness for Nicki. With him seemingly keeping it a secret, she didn't feel comfortable being completely open with people either. She nearly didn't have a baby shower out of fear that Atlas would explode if one of his friends or family members found out. Rae eventually convinced her to have a small celebration with only their side of the family.

One day, when Charlie Dettloff saw Nicki stopping over at Atlas's house while very visibly pregnant, he approached them. Charlie was friendly with Nicki during the couple years she lived next door to him with Atlas, and Charlie was surprised his neighbor hadn't told him Nicki was expecting a baby.

"Yeah, if it's even mine," Atlas quipped right in front of Nicki.

Charlie shut down the rude comment immediately, standing up to Tim in a way very few of his friends ever did.

"No, that's not OK," Charlie said. "We can't talk like that."

One winter night, midway through her pregnancy, Nicki heard from her parents that Atlas had requested a meeting with them at a Saint Paul restaurant. He hadn't informed Nicki of his plan, but she warned her parents he likely would bring up the topic of marriage because he recently had been relentless about it with her. Nicki hoped he would instead make an overture to mend his acrimonious relationship with Rae and Joe considering the baby would likely keep all of them in each other's lives.

Rae and Joe found the request odd because, over the course of Atlas and Nicki's relationship, Atlas had only attended one family dinner with them despite perpetual invitations. Atlas arrived late to the restaurant, ordered drinks instead of dinner, and quickly got to the point of his requested meeting.

"I would like to ask your permission to propose to your daughter," Atlas said.

Rae and Joe looked at each other. They knew what a volatile and terrible situation Nicki's relationship with Atlas had been, and they were under no illusions that a marriage would make it any better.

"She's an adult. You don't need my permission," Joe answered.

"Well then, I'm asking your blessing," Atlas said, adding that getting married before the baby arrives would be the right thing to do.

"We can't do that," Joe said.

Joe and Rae explained that they didn't believe marriage would resolve the issues between Atlas and Nicki. They suggested that Atlas address those problems before contemplating a proposal, emphasizing that existing issues don't resolve themselves with marriage. They tend to get harder.

When Atlas asked about the couple's biggest areas of concern, they candidly told him that they believed Atlas put himself and his Taekwondo studio before their daughter. And they hoped that once the baby was born, he would not put those things before his child.

Atlas grew more and more visibly dejected as the conversation continued. Joe and Rae cited examples of how Atlas seemed to abandon Nicki after Chantal's death and didn't support her during the hardest time of her life. They also brought up how, months later, instead of comforting Nicki during her first birthday without her twin, Atlas chose to go on an international vacation with an ex-girlfriend and her family.

"Tell me this. What do you think Nicole would say if you asked her to marry you?" Joe asked.

"I'm more than eighty percent sure she would say no," Atlas answered.

"Then why would you want to do this, considering those odds?" Joe asked.

"Because it's the right thing to do," Atlas said.

Rae and Joe tried to express that they believed the most important thing for their grandchild would be that he grew up in a healthy, happy home. If that meant growing up in two homes instead of one to accomplish that goal, then that would be better than having one home where there are problems.

Rae and Joe stayed calm throughout the conversation, even telling Atlas that he was an adult. They couldn't stop him. And they wouldn't do anything to stop Nicki if marrying him was what she really wanted. When Atlas persisted in asking for their blessing, the couple suggested they pause the conversation for a year and revisit it after he had worked on those relationship issues with their daughter.

As they got up to leave, Atlas—who had gotten drunk during the conversation—proceeded to the bar. The parents called Nicki on their drive home to let her know about the meeting and Atlas's insistence that he marry Nicki.

"I knew it!" Nicki responded.

When Nicki talked to Atlas the next day, however, he gave her a completely different version of how the meeting went.

"Your parents are racist," Atlas said. "Your dad looked at me and said he would never allow his daughter to marry someone of 'my kind.'"

"I know that's not true," Nicki responded. "Maybe you took something a certain way that they didn't mean."

"You're blind to it because you grew up with them. You're not going to see it," Atlas said. "Your dad is racist, and your mom co-signed it. I was so upset, I stayed at the bar and got hammered and had to call for a ride home."

Nicki followed up with her parents, who assured her that nothing they said during the meeting could even be misconstrued as a racist remark. She believed her mom and dad and saw it as an attempt by Atlas to ostracize her from her parents and drive her closer to him as a result. What it actually did was make it more awkward for her to continue contact with Atlas.

As a soon-to-be single mom, she knew she would need her full family support system.

As the weeks went by, Nicki's pregnancy extended beyond her June 9 due date. Despite Nicki being past due, Atlas decided to travel to an out-of-state Taekwondo tournament on the weekend of June 18 to 19. Even members of World Taekwondo Academy, who had only recently found out about Nicki's pregnancy, were surprised. Nicki had let go of hope that Atlas would be there for their son's birth. Rae helped her with everything about her birth plan as Nicki scheduled a time with her doctor to induce labor on Saturday, June 18.

The labor turned out to be very slow and difficult as Nicki fought a high fever and various complications. On Sunday evening, June 19, Nicki had still not given birth, allowing time for Atlas to arrive at the hospital. Soon, he began complaining about how long the process was taking and how tired he was from his tournament.

"Just go home. I'll call you when the birth is closer," Rae told him.

At about 3:15 a.m. on June 20, Rae called Atlas and suggested he hurry back. Upon his return, as a couple more hours passed and morning neared, Atlas again started asking the nurse how much longer it would take.

"I need to open up my gym soon. Do you think there's time to do that and make it back here?" Atlas asked the nurse. "Or will this be quick, and I can open it afterward?"

"I don't know what to tell you. Can't someone else open up your gym?" the nurse responded.

The situation at the hospital was already stressful for Nicki. Beyond the labor complications, the hospital's nursing staff was on strike, so the attending nurses were travel nurses from around the country who were not completely familiar with the hospital's systems. They were very supportive, however, and attempted to help Nicki with the tense situation with Atlas.

"Do you even want him here? Do you want me to kick him out?" the primary nurse, a Georgia resident, offered to Nicki after seeing the embarrassment on her face.

Once again, though, Nicki put herself in the role of peacekeeper, immediately envisioning how Atlas would hold it against her forever if she "prevented him from being there for the birth of his son."

"No, he can stay," she said.

Finally, just before 7:00 a.m., Nicki's son was born. Rae always said Nicki would make a great "boy mom" since she grew up a tomboy. Nicki had two possible names in mind, Callahan and Quentin, and she'd wanted to wait until she saw the baby to decide. As she held her boy for the first time, Nicki knew Callahan was the perfect fit.

The name-choosing process earlier in the pregnancy had already been stressful for Nicki. She tried to include Atlas in the decision, but he hated every name she proposed. The ones he came up with were too far outside the norm for Nicki's tastes—including the monicker he had chosen for himself, "Atlas."

"No, that's not even your name," Nicki said. "We're not naming the baby Atlas."

"Fine. Name him whatever you want to name him," Atlas said.

"OK, I will," she said.

Atlas came back with the suggestion they use Mark, his late father's first name, as the baby's middle name.

After resting in the hospital, Nicki filled out the naming paperwork, including the birth certificate. When she handed it to Atlas to sign, he saw "Callahan Mark Lenway" and began to freak out.

"I don't want Mark as the middle name," he said. "I changed my mind."

"Well, I like it, so now I'm keeping it," Nicki said.

With Mark as Callahan's middle name, his initials would be CML, the same as her late twin sister, Chantal Marie Lenway. Nicki thought it would be a great way to honor her sister. Plus, she was tired of accommodating Atlas despite his lack of helpfulness.

"You liked it five days ago. You're just being difficult."

"You don't even want my input. You don't care what I want. Your mom is in your ear, and you're just going to do what she wants," Atlas said right in front of Rae, who was sitting in the corner of the hospital room, trying to stay out of their conversation.

Atlas then directed his attention to the baby's last name. He was furious that Nicki had chosen Lenway instead of Amacher.

"I'm not going to let my kid have your racist parents' last name," Atlas added.

"Excuse me?" Rae piped in.

"You're not a part of this conversation," Atlas responded.

"Well, I am now. I want to know what you're talking about," Rae said. "I have never made a racist comment in my life."

Atlas claimed to have a recording of their restaurant conversation months earlier, after which he had made his first accusation of racism. He refused to play the alleged recording for Rae and Nicki. After he pivoted his grievances back toward Nicki, Rae left the hospital room. With the argument going nowhere, Atlas gave Nicki an ultimatum on the naming disagreement: If she insisted on giving their son her last name, he told her he would not sign the paperwork—the birth certificate or the right of parentage. And with that, the next morning, Nicki brought home Callahan Mark Lenway without the baby being "officially" named.

CHAPTER EIGHT

Nicki knew deep down she should have just signed and submitted the paperwork without Atlas. Yet, her mindset toward him remained focused on maintaining peace.

This is the father of my child. I'm going to have to deal with him. I don't want to do anything that's going to cause a big rift I'll have to deal with later, Nicki thought.

As the fighting over the name continued after leaving the hospital, Atlas suggested a "compromise."

"I'd be willing to live with Mark as the middle name as long as you change the last name to Amacher," Atlas said, emphasizing that "a son should have his father's last name."

With Atlas ultimately getting his way with his son, who received two names from Atlas's side of the family, he signed the paperwork that legally kept both parents in Callahan's life.

The timing of Cal's birth, eleven days after his due date, felt to Nicki like a sign from God. He was born one day before the third anniversary of Chantal's death, creating a happy memory in the space that was so sad. Nicki and her mother discussed how they wanted to ensure Cal's birthday would always be a joyous occasion without a 180-degree turn to sadness the next day.

The Lenways eventually decided to visit the Minnesota Zoo each year on the day after Callahan's birthday. That was one of Chantal's favorite places to visit throughout her life, and the tradition turned the anniversary day of grieving into a celebration of her life. The family would show Cal photos of Chan, teach him about her, and—once he learned to talk—answer questions he might have. That way, he would grow up honoring Chantal and "knowing" her the best he could in a positive way.

Nicki and Callahan. Photo furnished by Rae Lenway.

Before those plans were laid into place, Nicki's chief concern was figuring out how to co-parent with someone who was proving unreliable at best and potentially dangerous at worst.

She was hopeful Atlas would be present and have a real relationship with their son.

After taking eight weeks of maternity leave, Nicki prepared to return to work on a part-time basis at first. She still worked difficult overnight shifts, which presented an obvious challenge in caring for the sleeping baby. Atlas rarely visited Callahan during Nicki's maternity leave aside from lunches she arranged or trips to Atlas's gym that she took, so Atlas could see Cal between classes.

When Nicki started transitioning back to work, it was apparent that Atlas didn't even know his baby son or how to care for him at that point, so Nicki did not feel comfortable leaving Cal at Atlas's home for extended periods of time. She suggested to Atlas that he could take care of Cal during one of Nicki's two overnight shifts each week—which would be nothing more than monitoring the sleeping baby. However, Atlas taught evening fitness classes at his gym that ended later than the baby's bedtime, and he was unwilling to change the schedule.

Instead of driving Cal twenty-five minutes to World Taekwondo Academy, where the baby's routine would be disrupted every week, Nicki came up with an alternative. She was willing to put Cal to bed in her Northeast Minneapolis home and wait there until Atlas arrived before she headed to work. Atlas could then hang out at Nicki's house, go to sleep, give the baby a bottle in the middle of the night, and get up with Cal in the morning until Nicki returned home.

The new plan became a routine and expanded to multiple nights each week when Nicki resumed a full-time work schedule. Atlas began telling friends he had moved in with Nicki and that they were a family again. While he presented that charade to others, Atlas took several opportunities to try to rekindle his relationship with Nicki.

During that first year of single motherhood, Nicki wasn't completely closed off to the idea. Most of her friends had stable relationships with their partners, and those couples with kids were raising them together. If it somehow worked out between them, Nicki thought perhaps that's what would be best for Callahan. More often, however, incidents continued to remind Nicki that it was not meant to be.

On one Sunday night, when Atlas was supposed to watch Callahan, he didn't show up. Nicki couldn't reach him by call or text. Long after the arranged meeting time, and with the clock ticking before she needed to leave for work, Nicki arranged plans to drop off Cal at her parents' home, so they could watch him.

Just before walking out the door, Atlas answered the phone, and Nicki could tell he was under the influence of alcohol or drugs. Slurring his words, Atlas insisted he would be right there.

"He's my son. This is my commitment. I'm going to watch him," Atlas said, claiming he was completely sober.

"No, you're not," Nicki said. "I can tell you're in no state to watch him. Just sleep it off, and we'll figure it out."

Nicki was furious that Atlas, on a day that he knew well in advance he was supposed to care for their son, still put himself first and potentially created a dangerous scenario for all of them.

"I just can't rely on you," she said. "You care more about drinking and partying. You're acting like a twenty-year-old."

"You're keeping my son from me!" Atlas responded, attempting to turn the tables on her.

Atlas was adamant that he was going to get in his car and drive to Nicki's home. At that point, she felt responsible for his safety, too. If Atlas died in a car crash after that conversation, she couldn't bear to have that on her conscience.

Nicki swiftly packed up Cal to go to her parents' house, fearing that Atlas would arrive in a rage. She called Atlas's brother to let him know about the situation, asking him to stop Atlas from driving anywhere. Eventually, next-door neighbor Charlie called Nicki to let her know he had checked on Atlas and found him passed out with his cousin taking care of him.

Atlas later claimed he was in that state because of prescription painkillers reacting with mimosas he drank that morning at brunch. Nicki finally realized that despite her wanting to see the best in Atlas and years of making excuses for him, he would never be a reliable partner.

In addition, Nicki was repulsed to learn Atlas had a new roommate in the Saint Paul house that she shared with him for years. Colleen Larson, whom Nicki had met earlier as a young teen taking Taekwondo classes from Atlas, was renting his spare bedroom in the same unit of the duplex. She was eighteen years old and attending college at the University of St. Thomas in Saint Paul.

"That's gross. I'm not stupid; I know what that means," Nicki said after Atlas mentioned the living arrangement to her.

If there was one thing Nicki knew about Atlas, it's that he would not be living with a young woman unless they were sleeping together. Nicki was surprised to hear Colleen was eighteen and out of high school. She looked and acted younger, often tagging along with her little brother at World Taekwondo Academy.

"Oh my God, Lenway, it's not like that! How could you think like that? She's a student. I'm just providing her with a cheap place to live because she doesn't have much money," Atlas responded.

"OK, sure…" Nicki sarcastically said, eager to move on from those creepy thoughts.

Despite his young female roommate and whatever might have been going on between them, Atlas did not relent in his efforts to rekindle a formal relationship with Nicki, especially after she started letting him watch the baby in his own house.

"We should be together. Our son needs both of us. He needs us to be a family," Atlas would often say, forcing the conversation nearly every time she picked up Callahan in Saint Paul.

Finally, by spring 2017, Nicki felt the courage to present Atlas with finality.

"It's a no. I tried. It's never going to work. You are the same. You haven't changed. You keep saying you're changing, and you're going to be better, but you're the same person. I can't do this," Nicki told him.

Over the following months, Nicki remained focused on her son, her parenting, and her work. She wasn't putting herself out there into the dating world in any fashion, but during what was a violent summer in Minneapolis in 2017, she formed a friendship with a handsome patrol officer she kept seeing at crime scenes.

Nicki and Donovan together at a crime scene. Copyright Phillip Murphy.

Donovan Ford was a thirty-year-old, recently-divorced father of two, Nicki learned. She also shared details of her journey as a single parent at age twenty-eight—over which the two bonded. One role for patrol officers like Donovan is to keep crime scene investigators like Nicki safe while collecting evidence, so they can fully concentrate on their tasks. The two followed each other on Instagram, and Donovan messaged her after one of his long shifts at the scene of a fatal shooting on Nicki's day off.

"I thought I'd see you tonight," Donovan wrote, expressing disappointment about her absence. His message opened the door to more personal conversations as the two colleagues got to know each other via seemingly endless direct message Q and A sessions.

After a subsequent crime scene in which Nicki and her forensic scientist partner spent hours working with Donovan and his patrol partner, Donovan sent another Instagram DM.

"I know this is really lame to do it this way, but I don't have your number. I didn't think it would be appropriate to ask you at work, but I'd really like to get to know you. I know you're a single mom and don't have a lot of time, but maybe we could go out for coffee sometime."

CHAPTER NINE

Nicki and Donovan put a date on the calendar, three weeks away, on the first evening that their complicated work schedules and parenting arrangements aligned. However, a week early, Nicki's parents told her they were able to watch Callahan, excited that Nicki felt ready to get to know someone new. As it turned out, Donovan was available for the impromptu schedule change as well.

When Donovan told his work partner and good friend, Officer Mike Mays, about his upcoming date with Nicki, Mays teased that Donovan's date idea for dinner and a movie was too corny. Mays promised not to take credit as he planned for them a memorable day of indoor rock climbing followed by dinner at Donovan's favorite restaurant.

Donovan let Nicki know to wear athletic clothes while keeping their activity a surprise. He told her that he'd take her home to change and get ready before dinner, which Nicki appreciated because Rae was so excited for her daughter that she had bought her a new outfit to wear for the date.

Nicki was nervous about the date, and as they got to Vertical Endeavors, she revealed to Donovan that she was scared of heights. He apologized, worried that the surprise might be a bad idea. Nicki assured him she wanted to give it a try. The adrenaline-pumping activity brought them closer as Nicki conquered her fear.

That night at dinner, Nicki couldn't get over how genuine, kind, and understanding Donovan was. Talking to him was just so easy. They chatted about their kids, work, and their mutual love of Converse shoes—casually getting to know each other. There had been so much build-up to that day. Through long work shifts, where professionalism came first, they grew familiar with each other. Long direct message conversations, which were not face-to-face, also brought them closer.

Donovan made Nicki feel more valued and validated than she ever did in her relationship with Atlas. They couldn't wait to figure out the next time they could see each other, and they each went home with the euphoric excitement that comes at the beginning of a new relationship.

Nicki and Donovan on a date.
Photo furnished by Nicki Lenway.

Nicki's feelings were unfortunately mixed with anxiety about how Atlas would react when he found out since he hadn't given up on trying to woo her back. Even when their relationship was at its best, Atlas would twist situations to blame her for anything that went wrong. Nicki shared with Donovan the details of her tumultuous past with Atlas, even cautioning him that the situation might not be worth it.

"You might not want to step into my world," Nicki said.

"Everybody has baggage. We can figure it out. Let's not worry about that right now," Donovan assured her.

About a month into her new relationship with Donovan, Nicki broke the news to Atlas on a whim. While she was picking up Cal from Atlas's house, he blocked Nicki from leaving and went into his usual guilt-filled lectures advocating reconciliation.

"We need to be together for Cal. We need to be a family. You're not being a good mom if you're not trying to make this work," Atlas said.

"Look, I've moved on. I'm dating somebody," Nicki shot back. "You need to move on, too. This little fantasyland isn't going to happen. We are not a family. We are Cal's parents. We are not together, and we won't be together, and you know the reasons why. I'm not going to rehash this with you. It is what it is. Let's just move forward and be good parents to Cal. And figure out how to co-parent."

It was clear by Atlas's widening eyes that he was not expecting that news from Nicki. He then flew off the handle.

"That makes sense! Of course, you're going to be with somebody who's white. That's going to make your parents happy, and you'll do anything to please your parents. You were never going to end up with a Black guy," Atlas screamed.

While Atlas went on his rant, trying to bait Nicki by accusing her of acquiescing to her "racist" family's wishes, Nicki stayed quiet. Her silence irritated Atlas more.

"You don't have anything to say?" Atlas finally asked.

"Donovan is Black," Nicki succinctly answered.

"What? He's Black?" asked Atlas, clearly caught off guard.

"Yes, and my parents love him. It's always been a 'you' problem, not a race problem," Nicki replied.

After Nicki and Donovan started dating, her child exchanges with Atlas made Donovan nervous. He insisted that she always call him as soon as she left Atlas's home after each drop-off and pick-up, so he'd know she was safe. As she drove away from Atlas's house that day, she opened her call with, "Well…now Tim knows."

Donovan never referred to Tim as "Atlas," thinking it was goofy that a grown man outside of the entertainment industry would insist on using a "stage name." The couple laughed about Atlas's shock at Nicki dating a different Black man. But Nicki and Donovan misread how, beyond his initial reaction, Atlas would take the news. They were hopeful it would be the prompt that finally made him move on with his life as well. Donovan's emergence into Atlas's orbit only made him dig in harder.

When Nicki's work shifts started including more afternoons and evenings, Callahan began to spend more nights with Atlas. One night, after finishing a training session about ten minutes away from her house, Nicki was looking forward to getting home, relaxing, and getting some sleep. She planned to pick up Cal from Atlas's house in the morning. When she got to her front door, Nicki noticed her deadbolt was unlocked—a sign something was off.

That's really weird. I always lock it, Nicki thought as she hesitantly stepped inside her home.

As she walked in, Nicki saw the entrance was filled with red roses and petals everywhere. Nicki stopped and shook her head.

This wasn't Donovan. He knows I hate roses.

Nicki had given Atlas a house key during the period when he would sleep at her house to watch Cal during her overnight work shifts. She thought he had returned it. By the look of the grand gesture in front of her, however, it appeared Atlas still had that key.

I can't believe this mothereffer came into my house while I was gone, Nicki thought.

Feeling invaded, Nicki began noticing little notes scattered among the roses. The notes gave clues to find hidden gifts—an apparent scavenger hunt. The clues led Nicki to a bottle of Jameson whiskey in the clothes dryer in the basement, as well as a picture frame and other random home decor items hidden in her house. Everywhere she looked, there were more roses—one hundred in all.

As she made her way through the house, Nicki called Donovan to vent about the intrusiveness of Atlas's dramatic display. After getting off the phone, she continued talking aloud to herself.

"And he doesn't even know that I hate roses," Nicki scoffed to herself, incredulous about the irony in Atlas's latest attempt to win her back.

"I can hear what you're saying," Atlas said as he sheepishly walked out of Nicki's guest bedroom holding a bouquet of roses, giving her a jump scare.

Atlas was supposed to be watching Cal. Nicki had no idea he was still in her house as she walked through his scavenger hunt.

"What are you doing here?" Nicki gasped. "This is completely inappropriate. I didn't give you permission to be in my home. In what way did you think it would be appropriate to do something like this when you know I'm in a relationship with somebody else?"

"I'm sorry," Atlas said, handing Nicki back her house key.

When she asked Atlas about Cal, he told Nicki that a young male Taekwondo student was watching their son at Atlas's house.

"You're supposed to be watching our son, but instead, you took the opportunity to break into my house because you knew I wouldn't be home? How irresponsible are you?" Nicki asked.

Before she could delve much deeper into the violation she felt by his actions, Atlas began portraying himself as the victim.

"It's pretty clear how you feel about me," he said, near tears.

The next day, Nicki called her dad to change the locks on her home. Reminders of the incident periodically arose, however. At one point, Atlas asked Nicki about an item belonging to Donovan that was kept in a private drawer in her house. Another time, Atlas texted Nicki a photo he snapped on his camera phone showing a framed photograph of Nicki and Donovan she kept on a dresser.

In August 2017, Atlas's brother Jesse was getting married in Stillwater, Minnesota, about a half-hour from Minneapolis. Atlas's mother, who lived in Indiana, and several other family members insisted that Callahan be there. Nicki was uncomfortable sending her now one-year-old toddler to an event like that without her, especially since Atlas had a role in the wedding that would divide his attention. After discussing with Donovan, Nicki agreed she would bring Cal to the wedding and then leave with him after the toast.

With Atlas seated at the head table, Nicki barely needed to interact with him during the day, but when she did, it was obvious that many of Atlas's friends and family members still thought the two were together and attending the wedding as a couple.

"This will be you guys soon. Maybe you two will be next," some of Atlas's friends said in passing.

As is typical at every wedding, the photographer rushed to gather different combinations of family members for portraits. Callahan posed with Atlas's mom and other family members, and then the photographer looked at Nicki and Atlas and said, "OK, now you guys."

Nicki felt extremely uncomfortable, but she didn't want to cause a negative disruption. Nicki looked down at Callahan and smiled as the boy slowly walked toward them and reached up. Atlas smiled and put his left arm around Nicki's waist, pulling her close to him as he reached down to Cal with his other hand.

Oh, no. This isn't good, Nicki thought to herself as soon as the photo was taken. Sure enough, the photograph seemed to depict a young, attractive couple in a loving embrace, gazing down at their toddler son. Nicki immediately thought about how misleading the photo would look to Donovan. She just didn't predict when and how he would see it.

Weeks later, Atlas somehow obtained Donovan's personal cell phone number—no easy feat because police officers take steps to maintain their privacy. Donovan's phone buzzed, and there was the photograph, along with a message from Atlas:

"You are truly a shitty person, messing with a girl that is obviously not in her right mind. You are getting in the way of a family coming together. It's obvious you have no respect, and the word family might even be foreign to you. Be sure to stay away from my son."

"What is this picture?" Donovan asked Nicki, confused.

Nicki explained the circumstances behind the photograph.

"I get it," he responded. "I'm not happy about it, but under the circumstances, I get it."

Enraged that Donovan didn't respond to his bait, Atlas continued his barrage of calls and texts to Donovan, who never answered or responded.

"I suggest you call back. This is Atlas. You have one hour to call back. To 'serve and protect'...you must believe in 'to homewreck and disrespect'...that, or 'to serve' means something totally different to you! I wait for you to man up and call me. 1hr," one text message said.

"I'll keep this pretty easy for you. You can either call me and man up, or I can come find you and talk to you in person at your work or at your house; it's really your call. I don't blame you 100% for things that have happened, but I do wanna talk to you," another text read.

Eventually, in those text messages, Atlas referred to Nicki as his "NOW ex-girlfriend," but his threatening tone remained as he insulted Donovan and threatened his career and family life. Atlas had learned the name of Donovan's MPD partner, Mike Mays, through his own friends at the Saint Paul Police Department. Atlas used that information to concoct a narrative that Donovan called Nicki a "side piece" when talking with fellow officers.

Through their brief interactions during child pickups and drop-offs, Atlas revealed to Nicki that he knew what shift Donovan worked and at which precinct as well as the address where Donovan's ex-wife and children lived. Donovan was frightened for their safety.

At one point, Nicki received a voicemail from a woman who sounded like she was reading from a script: "I've been dating Officer Donovan Ford for several months." The message upset Nicki until she and Donovan analyzed it together and realized how odd it was that the woman would robotically say "Officer

Donovan Ford" instead of just Donovan. They assumed the woman was someone Atlas had put up to it.

Another clearly staged scenario played out right after Donovan got off the phone with Nicki following a parenting exchange at Atlas's house. After talking with Nicki by phone per their custom, Donovan canceled an incoming call from Atlas, sending him to voicemail.

"What's going on, Donovan? I've got Nicki here sitting next to me," Atlas's voicemail message began. "Why don't you give me a call back, so we can all have a conversation? You calling her a 'side piece' and all those other things you've called her is pretty messed up."

In the voicemail, Atlas threatened to send out incriminating information about Donovan and Nicki unless he "manned up" and stopped "hiding behind the badge."

While the threats regarding Donovan's relationship with Nicki were concerning enough, Atlas's final text message to Donovan about Callahan was ominous: "And to be clear…I will NEVER be ok with you around my son."

CHAPTER TEN

Over the winter, Nicki's entire family quickly grew very fond of Donovan. He celebrated Thanksgiving and Christmas with them, which was something Atlas never did. Atlas always made excuses to avoid the Lenways. When Donovan's father came to visit from Colorado, he came right over to meet Nicki's parents and even spent time with her grandparents. The relief on their faces to see Nicki in such a positive and healthy relationship was apparent to her.

As their relationship grew stronger, so did Atlas's desperation. Nicki's parents planned a trip to Mexico in March 2018, inviting Nicki and Cal to join them. As the trip drew closer, Atlas gave Nicki an ultimatum. He told her to break up with Donovan by March 17, the day the Lenways would fly to Mexico, or Atlas would kill himself.

Atlas's justification was that he didn't want Callahan to grow up in a "broken family," so he had decided to "sacrifice himself" to prevent the "confusion" that two father figures in his life would cause Cal.

"You don't think it's messed up that you would do that to Cal? That's messed up!" Nicki responded when Atlas first set the "deadline."

"He's young. He won't remember. And you will just replace me anyway," Atlas responded. "You have until March 17 to make your decision."

Despite the ongoing headaches Atlas was causing, Nicki felt heartbroken by the ultimatum and how Cal would be affected for the rest of his life if his dad followed through with his threat.

After learning of her relationship with Donovan, Atlas threatened suicide multiple times. One time, he relayed a story back to Nicki about how he overdosed on prescription pills because he was so upset and that two friends showed up at his house and saved his life.

Another time, in front of Nicki and Callahan, when he could tell his pleas for Nicki to leave Donovan and come back to him were not working, Atlas pulled a loaded handgun out of his nightstand drawer and put it in his mouth.

"Might as well pull the trigger," Atlas said as Nicki cried and pleaded with him to put down the gun. "Everything you're doing is killing me anyway."

Nicki felt sure Atlas was going to kill her, then himself, but she somehow convinced Atlas to put the gun down.

With hindsight, it can be easier to look back on instances like those as idle threats motivated by Atlas's desire to always get what he wants. At the time, though, the possibility of Atlas following through felt very real to Nicki. She talked about it with her mom and her best friend, Anya, at length.

"He's not going to do that. He's a narcissist. He'll never do that," Rae and Anya would both tell her.

"But if he does, I'm going to feel so guilty," Nicki would respond. "I don't want to be the reason he does something like that."

On March 16, the day before Atlas's deadline, Nicki brought Cal to Atlas's Taekwondo studio to have lunch with him. She hoped putting Cal literally in front of Atlas would help him grasp the gravity of his plans.

"I want you to think about your son and how that's going to impact him. Don't make dumb decisions just because of a former romantic relationship. This is your kid," she said.

Nicki told Atlas she had no intention of breaking up with Donovan. She refused to feel like a hostage to Atlas and his threats to control their lives. He couldn't force her into a relationship any more than she could compel him to do anything.

"This isn't healthy," she told him.

Atlas proceeded to show Nicki his will, which left all of his assets to her and Callahan in the event of his death. Atlas told Nicki he would rather they benefit from his life insurance policy than Cal grow up in two households.

"I'm a man of my word," Atlas said, indicating that he intended to follow through with his threat.

The Lenways' vacation in Mexico was shadowed by fears of what Atlas would do. Nicki did not have cell phone service, but each time she was in a spot with Wi-Fi, she would check her phone and download a barrage of messages from Atlas about his continued plans for suicide. Once away from Wi-Fi service, Nicki would feel overwhelmed with anxiety until she again read through a dump of messages. Atlas's clients and friends also began texting Nicki, worried about Atlas's depressive state.

Atlas finally wrote that he had rented a hotel room under a fake name so that no one could find him. He said he had his gun with him and that Nicki wouldn't hear from him again.

For more than twenty-four hours after that last text, Atlas did not reply to anything Nicki or anyone else wrote—conveying the possibility that this time, he really did kill himself. Nicki couldn't help but worry for his safety and her son's future. Finally, Atlas wrote Nicki another message saying he had changed his mind. He was still alive, and he said they could talk about it when Nicki and Cal returned from Mexico.

After the vacation, the next time Nicki saw Atlas for a parenting exchange, Atlas tried to prove the validity of his suicide threat by showing her a number of letters he had written and planned to leave behind for friends and family along with a receipt for the hotel room he'd rented. Atlas claimed he really did check in under an alias, but before he pulled the trigger, he saw a commercial on TV that featured a nuclear family. That gave him an epiphany. He thought it was a sign from God that he, Nicki, and Cal would still somehow end up together.

Unbelievable, Nicki thought.

After all that, he still twisted the events into an attempt to reconcile with Nicki. She felt angered and manipulated by Atlas's cruel tactic, staining her family vacation while continuing to blame his actions on her. It was clear that Atlas simply could not accept that Nicki had moved on. His actions would soon become more threatening toward her.

One Saturday morning in June 2018, after a long shift at work, Nicki was trying to get some sleep when she awoke to a knock at her door. It was one of her neighbors, who sheepishly told Nicki, "Hey, I'm so sorry to wake you, but there is something on your garage that you might want to see."

Nicki walked outside to the back alley where her detached garage and all of her neighbors' garages were located. The alley was bustling because the neighbors were preparing to hold a garage sale. And there, written in bright orange spray paint on Nicki's garage door: "Slut 4 Cops."

Nicki's defaced garage door. Photo furnished by Nicki Lenway.

"I just thought you'd want to know," the neighbor sympathetically said.

Nicki flushed red with embarrassment and anger and opened the garage door so that the garage sale shoppers and the rest of her neighbors wouldn't be able to see it. There was never any doubt in her mind that Atlas had done it, sometime between 10:00 p.m. when she got home from work and 8:00 a.m. when the neighbor knocked. She didn't have any surveillance cameras, however, and Atlas was supposed to be at his house watching Cal during that time. Nicki called her dad.

"What do I do? How do you get this off?" she desperately asked.

Joe picked up some supplies and met Nicki at her house. Together, they scrubbed the spray paint with cleaner until it looked like an illegible blob. Joe also brought paint to redo the entire garage door, but they decided to tackle that project another time.

In the meantime, Atlas had begun bombarding Nicki with calls and texts, telling her he needed to get something from her house. She could already sense he was looking for an excuse to "find" the garage door graffiti.

Finally, after her dad left, Nicki responded to Atlas and told him he could stop by. First, she opened the garage door again so that Atlas wouldn't be able to see the blob of paint. That didn't work. Soon after arriving and parking in the alley, Atlas pounded on Nicki's front door.

"What's going on? I can see what's written on your garage," Atlas said.

"Oh, my God, what are you talking about? Why did you touch my garage? Why did you close the door?" Nicki asked.

"It's obvious what it says. *Slut 4 Cops*, Nicki? Your lifestyle is endangering Cal," Atlas said.

"You fucking did this!" Nicki said. "What are you talking about, 'My lifestyle?' There is no way you can read what that says."

"Everyone knows Donovan has all sorts of women on the side. You should ask him which one of them was crazy enough to do this," Atlas said.

"I'm not stupid. I know it was you or that you had someone else do it," Nicki repeated.

Atlas then pivoted from blaming a jealous woman to suggesting that another officer must have painted the graffiti.

"The color of the paint is clearly the same as officers carry in their squad cars. How can you even accuse me of that?" Atlas said before revealing his true intention in this latest ordeal. "You aren't safe to live here. You're putting Cal at risk. Both of you should live with me until this gets sorted out."

"You're nuts. I'm in a relationship. Why would I move in with you?" Nicki asked.

"No, not like that," Atlas said, feigning surprise at the suggestion he was proposing another reconciliation. "Just until you're safe. You can stay in a different bedroom, and you can just live with me until everything is safe again."

"I'm not doing that. I don't feel safe with you. And I know you did this!" Nicki responded. "You need to go."

Atlas's attempts to drive a wedge between Nicki and Donovan continued to fail. Nicki didn't believe any of Atlas's lies about Donovan simultaneously dating other women or not taking his relationship with Nicki seriously. But Atlas thought one last grand gesture could win her back.

Later that summer, Atlas was planning a trip to Las Vegas for his friend Taiwan's fortieth birthday. He invited Nicki to go with him. She told him that it was clearly not appropriate to ask as she had been in a relationship with Donovan for over a year. Nicki made it clear she would not be going, but Atlas was relentless. He kept trying to convince Nicki that it wouldn't be a romantic situation and that she was friends with many of the other people who would be there.

"Even if I wasn't dating Donovan, and even if you and I got along better, I would still have reservations about going to Las Vegas with you after what happened last time we were there," Nicki added, referencing the 2014 trip where Atlas kicked the elevator door and snapped in their room.

When Nicki refused to entertain the idea, Atlas started asking his friends to contact Nicki and try to convince her to go. That only irritated her further.

"Hey, us girls have to stick together. You gotta come, so I have someone to hang with. Don't leave me alone," Taiwan's wife, Cindy, texted Nicki.

"Look, I don't know what he's told you or tried to convey about our relationship, but we are strictly co-parenting at this point," Nicki responded, hoping Atlas's friends would back off and stop exacerbating the situation.

As the day of the flight drew near, in a last-ditch attempt, Atlas told Nicki that he had bought her a plane ticket anyway. She did not go to the airport. Even then, Atlas's friends messaged Nicki from Las Vegas, expressing concern about how dejected Atlas seemed.

That Friday, while stewing in Las Vegas, Atlas signed paperwork in front of a notary public to send back to Minnesota. A couple of days later, those papers were served to Nicki. She couldn't believe it. After all the begging. After all the threats. After all the manipulation. Nicki thought Atlas had run out of ways to try to control her. He hadn't. He filed for sole custody of Callahan.

CHAPTER ELEVEN

At about 8:30 in the evening on Wednesday, August 22, 2018, Nicki dropped off Cal at Atlas's Saint Paul home before her overnight work shift as had become their routine over the course of the past year. A contentious back-and-forth argument, no different than what occurred during every parenting exchange, then commenced. As Nicki walked from Atlas's front door back to her car, a man stepped forward and handed her some paperwork, saying, "Nicole Lenway? You've been served."

The situation seemed so absurd that Nicki believed at first it was another one of Atlas's staged attempts to get under her skin. She looked down at the paperwork, which was titled "Petition to Establish Custody and Parenting Time."

Could this possibly be real?

Despite all the co-parenting drama Nicki endured during the first two years of Callahan's life, she always made a point of involving Atlas in their son's life. If she hadn't conceded to Atlas's naming preferences, he might never have signed the recognition of parentage. At several points, it seemed like Atlas would not have ever seen Cal if Nicki hadn't driven the child up to Atlas's Taekwondo studio. After all those efforts she made to include Atlas as a parent, did he now really want to take her son away from her?

Over the previous several months, Atlas had made threats of that sort, which seemed more like unhealthy attempts to reconcile. They usually came in the context of, "If you don't break up with Donovan and do what's best for Cal and come together as a family, then I'll be left with no choice but to make sure you never see him again." During those particular fights, the threats didn't seem like something Atlas would actually carry out. Nicki completely financially supported Cal. Since there was no custody arrangement, Atlas was not paying child support. And he certainly didn't voluntarily pitch in.

"Oh, believe me, Lenway, I have plenty of dirt on you," Atlas would tell Nicki, threatening to "get her fired." Again, Nicki didn't think he'd go that far because, without her salary, Cal would suffer.

Nicki sent the petition to her uncle, who was a lawyer, and he told her the paperwork very much appeared to be real. Atlas was asking a family court judge to award him legal and physical custody of Callahan, with the boy's primary residence being Atlas's house. Nicki's uncle told her she needed to retain a family law attorney and prepare for a contentious legal fight. Most importantly, she needed to get Cal back as soon as possible and keep the boy away from Atlas until a judge weighed in on the issue, and they had a custody agreement in writing.

Trying to remain calm, Nicki contacted Atlas about arranging for pick-up the next day, as planned, after her overnight shift. Sure enough, Atlas refused to turn Cal over. He took the opportunity to complain about his parenting time and how it revolved around Nicki's work schedule. Rather than argue, Nicki did her best to pacify Atlas. She feared he would never give Cal back.

Thursday turned to Friday, and Friday turned to Saturday, and Atlas continued to refuse Nicki's gentle requests to pick up her son. Dread began to overwhelm her. He warned her not to try getting him that afternoon as he had Callahan at a friend's pool party.

"If you try to come, I've already informed them to call the cops," Atlas told Nicki over the phone. "You can't take my son from me."

Finally, on Sunday morning, Atlas allowed Nicki to pick up Cal. Upon Nicki walking in the door, Atlas snapped when Cal ran to his mom for a hug after not seeing her in days. Atlas complained that he wanted more time to finish feeding Cal breakfast and getting him ready. Then, Atlas got in Nicki's face, and his language turned vile.

"You slut," he said. "Who knows how many other cops you're sleeping with at this point?"

That word stung because, despite the countless insults and demeaning things Atlas had said to Nicki over the years, that was the first time he'd called her a slut to her face. She immediately thought of the "Slut 4 Cops" graffiti that Atlas so emphatically claimed he had nothing to do with.

As Atlas continued vulgar insults and complaints about their existing informal co-parenting schedule, Nicki did not engage. She started directing her attention toward their two-year-old boy.

"How's your morning going?" Nicki asked Cal, who was standing right there as his father spewed venom at Nicki.

Atlas grew even more enraged that Nicki was ignoring his insults.

"Get out of my house," Atlas said. "I'll bring Cal out when he's ready."

Nicki followed his instruction, praying that Atlas would follow through and bring the boy outside to her. Minutes later, when Atlas finally carried Cal to Nicki's SUV and placed him in the car seat, she felt momentary relief. But then, Atlas wouldn't close the door.

"Please shut the door, so I can leave," Nicki pleaded, but Atlas refused.

The incident was very similar to something that had happened earlier that year outside Atlas's Taekwondo studio. On Valentine's Day, when Nicki picked up Cal, Atlas brought a few gifts out to her car and slid into the passenger seat next to her. Nicki was furious about the blatant disrespect Atlas showed for her seven-month relationship with Donovan.

In response, Atlas degraded Nicki and refused to get out of the car. Feeling trapped and scared, Nicki tried pushing Atlas out from her driver's seat—to no effect. She got out and tried pulling Atlas out of the car but couldn't budge him.

Atlas then quickly got out on his own, unbuckled Callahan, and started carrying him back into the studio, telling Nicki it wasn't safe for their child to be with her while she was "so emotional." Atlas had threatened multiple times by that point that he'd take Cal away from Nicki, and she'd never see him again. So, in that moment, flashes of fear of losing her son forever overcame her. After crying and pleading with Atlas, he finally let Nicki and Cal leave.

As that scenario began to unfold again, this time with a pending custody case looming, Nicki collected herself. Hoping to avoid another Valentine's Day scene, Nicki calmly told Atlas again, "Please close the door, so I can leave."

"Maybe if you weren't such a slut, your lifestyle choices wouldn't have such an impact on your son," Atlas said.

Then, the impact of Atlas's repeated use of that word was reflected from the back seat.

"Slut, slut, slut," Callahan mimicked from his car seat.

"Nope, nope, nope," Nicki said to the impressionable toddler, trying to shush him before he repeated any more inappropriate words he heard from his dad. Turning back to Atlas, Nicki said, "My 'lifestyle choices' are affecting Cal? Look what you're doing to him right now. That's completely inappropriate to say in front of your son."

"I'm not saying anything that's not true," Atlas responded.

Atlas continued using the word as he refused to shut the door, escalating his badgering of Nicki and referring to her relationship with Donovan as a "lifestyle choice" that was somehow damaging to their son.

"Everything's about you, and you're so selfish," Atlas said. "It's just about you and your job."

"If you don't shut the door right now, I'm calling the police," Nicki finally said.

"I have lots of friends in the Saint Paul Police Department. Let's see where that gets you," Atlas snapped back.

Nicki pulled out her phone and began dialing. Seeing that, Atlas finally stepped away from the car and shut Callahan's door. As she drove away from Atlas's Saint Paul house, Nicki called Donovan, crying about the clear impact the dysfunctional situation was having on Callahan. She didn't just fear losing Cal, though. She was afraid for her own life, and it was long past due that she stopped internalizing those fears.

Nicki knew she needed to act quickly to protect herself and Cal. A coworker at the Minneapolis Police Department—someone she trusted—told her to go straight to the Domestic Abuse

Service Center at the Hennepin County Government Center and apply for an order for protection. If a judge deemed it an emergency, the order could be signed on the same day. Rae and Anya had urged Nicki to file for a protection order in the past, but Nicki had resisted. She didn't want her private life bleeding into her work. Her coworkers didn't know the depths of her problems with Atlas, and she didn't want the drama to become MPD gossip. Finally, however, Nicki saw just now how necessary that order had become.

As soon as she started sharing her situation with the advocate at the center, emotion began pouring out of Nicki. She hoped the court system could strip away the charming facade and charismatic persona of "Atlas" and look at Tim Amacher for who he really was. She began by spelling out her experience of getting trapped by Tim while picking up Cal.

"I am filing this order now because Tim is getting to the point that he is abusing me in front of Cal, and that makes me even more scared of him because he is willing to inflict fear onto me with Cal present," Nicki wrote in her affidavit.

Nicki gave an overview of their history, including incidents where Tim physically harmed her or made her afraid. That included Tim dragging Nicki by her ponytail after she tried to leave his house in September 2015 as well as Tim's escalating behavior after she started dating Donovan.

"I haven't a problem with him and Cal having time together. I want them to have a relationship. However, Tim is causing me serious fear for my safety at the expense of our son. I thought that when I left him, he would leave me alone, and we could co-parent in a healthy way. However, when we do parenting exchanges, Tim will use those moments as ways to hurt or scare me," Nicki wrote.

Nicki requested that the judge order Tim to contact her by phone only for child medical emergencies and otherwise use email—no more than once per day—for parenting time scheduling purposes only. She suggested they decide on a local police department as the location for parenting exchanges.

The victim services advocate empathetically listened and helped Nicki organize the escalation of her emotionally abusive and sometimes physically abusive relationship with Tim. He then prepared her with a grave warning.

"This could make things worse," he said, alluding to how abusers sometimes react to an attempt to obtain a court order. "Just be aware that this could be very dangerous for you, but it is one of the only things you can do to hold him accountable."

Immediately after leaving the government center, Nicki and her parents installed cameras at her Northeast Minneapolis house and grabbed what she needed for her and Cal to stay with them until they received clarity from the court.

Nicki received notification that a judge ruled in her favor, determining that Nicki's petition articulated an immediate danger of domestic abuse. The judge issued an emergency order for protection and scheduled a hearing with testimony and evidence if Tim chose to fight it. The judge agreed to Nicki's proposed contact restrictions and ordered Tim to stay at least three quarters of a mile away from Nicki, her house, the Minneapolis crime lab where she worked, and Donovan's house.

Nicki met with an attorney, Stacy Lofgren, who emphasized how important it would be to stay organized and detail-oriented when dealing with someone like Tim. The order for protection would not go into effect until Tim was served with the paperwork. Unfortunately, a sheriff's deputy was unable to find Tim immediately. Nicki avoided Tim's calls as he left nonstop messages demanding to see his son.

After canceling an August 30 dentist appointment for Cal to buy another day for Tim to be served, Nicki decided to keep an August 31 doctor appointment. Tim knew about it, and despite having never gone along to appointments in the past, under the circumstances, Nicki had no doubt he would show up. So, Nicki brought her mother along for support.

"What are you doing here?" Tim immediately asked Rae.

"Because she doesn't feel safe, and she doesn't want to be here with you," said Rae, who wasn't shy about calling out Tim.

Nicki had to assure the nurse that she wanted her mother present after Tim asked her to remove Rae. An awkward hour-long experience at the clinic then commenced with Tim badgering Nicki in the waiting room, demanding to know when he could take Cal. As soon as a nurse or doctor entered the room, Tim's mood or demeanor changed 180 degrees, and he acted sociable, charming, and even cracked jokes. Once Tim, Nicki, Rae, and Callahan were alone again, Tim resumed tormenting Nicki.

"You need to let me take Cal. I haven't seen him. I'm taking him when I leave here," Tim shouted as Nicki and Cal both started physically shaking in fear.

"Please don't do this in front of your son," Rae pleaded with Tim as Nicki looked down, not knowing how to respond. "Just email Nicki later. Don't be doing this in front of your son."

When the insufferable experience was nearing a close, Tim abruptly left the room. He came back and told Nicki and Rae that he had just gotten off the phone with his lawyer. They were both astounded by what Tim said next.

"You better convince your daughter to come back to me, or she's going to regret it," Tim said to Rae before turning to Nicki. "And you know exactly what I'm talking about, Lenway."

Tim had told Nicki numerous times that if she didn't reconcile with Tim, he would take everything from her—Callahan, her job, her friendships, and her reputation. Plus, he promised to bankrupt her and her parents with legal costs.

"The door is still open. Do the right thing before it's too late," Tim said.

The very next day, Tim was finally served with the order for protection, and he contacted his attorney to file for an identical one against Nicki. A judge denied his proposed emergency order and set a court date for Tim to make further arguments. When she received the paperwork filed by Tim, Nicki began to see how he was willing to bend the facts and outright lie on sworn statements to try to get what he wanted.

"At our last doctor's appointment on 8-31-18, Nicki and her mother verbally assaulted and threatened me to the point where I had to contact my lawyer and leave," Tim wrote.

Tim claimed that at the appointment, Nicki told him, "I am not going to let you see my son," and "I will have Donovan 'take care' of you."

Regarding Rae, Tim continued his false claims of racism, quoting Nicki's mom as saying to him, "It will be two white ladies versus you. Who do you think they will believe?"

Besides Tim's re-imagining of the arguments at the doctor's appointment, Tim revealed in his petition a trump card he had been holding over Nicki. On the day before he left for Las Vegas after Nicki made it clear she would not go on the trip with him, Tim filed a report with the White Bear Lake Police Department—in the city where his successful taekwondo studio was located—accusing Nicki of domestic abuse. The police officer who took the report believed him.

CHAPTER TWELVE

At about 5:30 p.m. on August 16, 2018, just twelve hours before his flight to Las Vegas, Tim called White Bear Lake Police to let them know he was preparing to serve his ex-partner with custody papers. He asked to speak to an officer about his "fears" of how Nicki was going to respond in the coming days.

"It's not easy being a man and in an abusive relationship," Tim told Officer Nathan Hook, who had driven to Tim's Taekwondo studio to hear his concerns.

Leaning back in his chair inside his small office at World Taekwondo Academy wearing black martial arts pants and a gray tank top, Tim solemnly proceeded to paint himself as a victim of physical abuse throughout his relationship with Nicki.

"There's a numerous amount of times where she's been either physical or verbal with me right inside this office," Tim told the wide-eyed police officer.

Officer Hook, a New Zealand native who made a career change to law enforcement in his forties, had his sights set on becoming a detective within the small suburban police force. He activated his body camera and eagerly prompted Tim to continue his narrative.

"I've been trying to get my family back together for two years now," Tim continued, telling the officer that "infidelity" on Nicki's part had complicated his efforts, and now he could no longer take the "abuse."

As Tim began to see Officer Hook's complete willingness to believe him, Tim leaned into a veil of reluctance to share details, forcing the officer to empathetically pull them from him. While describing their informal co-parenting arrangement, Tim insinuated that he was Callahan's primary caretaker.

"Sometimes it's sixty percent of the week. Some weeks I have him seventy percent of the week. The problem is, I never know when I'm going to have him," Tim said, claiming that Nicki would frequently drop Cal off unexpectedly or with short notice because of her work schedule and that she refused to plan a parenting schedule with him.

"That does make it challenging!" Officer Hook responded.

As Tim began going through a laundry list of abuse claims, Officer Hook validated everything Tim said.

"OK, so, she's kind of a Jekyll and Hyde character who—under stress—blows up on you, becomes violent, and then she seems to regret her actions and goes back to being nice again," Officer Hook said as he visualized the scenarios described by Tim.

Tim told the officer he wanted to press charges against Nicki for one incident in particular. Tim claimed that three months earlier, on May 27, Nicki intentionally ran over his foot with her vehicle while he was holding Cal.

Nicki remembered the incident well and had thought to herself since that day that Tim might try to use it against her in some way. She had just dropped off Cal at Tim's gym at about 11:30

a.m. As usual, Tim began criticizing Nicki and commenting on her relationship with Donovan. He walked up to Nicki's open car window while holding Cal and continued chirping at her.

"I need to leave. I'm not having this conversation again," Nicki said as Tim stepped back.

Nicki began backing up, her head turned around, looking out her rear windshield, when Tim smacked the hood of the car as hard as he could with one hand. Startled, Nicki slammed on the brakes.

"You're on my foot! Pull forward," Tim said.

Nicki quickly put the car back into drive and lurched forward a foot or so before throwing the shifter into park, at which point Tim flopped backward onto the ground, still holding Cal. Tim then got up and walked into his gym with the boy. Nicki exited her vehicle and followed them inside.

"Did I really run over your foot? What's going on? If I did, you need to go to the hospital," she said, emphasizing the damage a heavy SUV such as hers would do to someone's foot.

"No, no. I don't want to get you in trouble or anything with your job," Tim oddly responded.

"Why would I get in trouble?" Nicki asked.

Tim refused to seek medical care, and he wouldn't show Nicki his alleged injury either. That led Nicki to believe he had staged the entire thing. Tim resumed teaching classes as Nicki left the Taekwondo studio and called Donovan on her way to work.

"He's going to use this in some way," Nicki told her boyfriend, suspicious but unable to foresee Tim's angle. "I don't know how, but I know he's going to use this."

Three months after the incident, Nicki learned through an email from her boss, Shannon Johnson, the director of the Minneapolis Crime Lab, that she was being criminally charged. Shannon had forwarded the message she received, which notified her that the White Bear Lake City Attorney had decided to charge Nicki with two counts of domestic abuse. These misdemeanor charges alleged that Nicki intended to cause fear and harm to Tim by striking him with her vehicle.

"Sorry, we have to forward this to internal affairs. It is what it is," Shannon wrote to Nicki.

Shannon was a supportive boss who knew some of what Nicki was dealing with. Yet, there is a lot of bureaucracy within any large police department, and those allegations meant a lot of trouble for Nicki at her workplace. They needed to alter her job duties while the criminal case and the corresponding internal affairs investigation proceeded.

Nicki hired a criminal defense attorney, Kelli Gaborsky, in hopes that she could get the prosecutor to dismiss the case. Not only did White Bear Lake City Attorney Luke McClure refuse to drop the charges, but he also suggested that Nicki should accept a plea deal. The prosecutor wanted to charge the case because of a child being involved. In addition, he justified the decision because he certainly would've pursued the case if the genders were reversed. McClure believed Tim's story because of all the additional anecdotes of "abuse" Tim had told Officer Hook in his initial report.

Tim began with a re-imagined version of the time he trapped Nicki in her car in the parking lot of his gym on Valentine's Day. Tim told the officer he had slid into Nicki's passenger seat to discuss scheduling issues caused by Nicki's job.

"Then she said, 'I'll just make you pay child support, or you won't see him at all,'" Tim said.

"OK, so she threatened to deny you access to Callahan, OK," Officer Hook responded.

"I said I just really want to know the schedule. I even brought up going to a mediator. Then she just lost it and started hitting me," Tim said, claiming he then grabbed Callahan from his car seat to remove him from the situation as Nicki continued her assault.

In an even more unbelievable story, Tim described Nicki, on December 30, 2017, pulling Tim's loaded handgun from his top drawer, pointing at him, and saying, "I wish you were dead." Tim told Officer Hook that Callahan was in the room at the time, and he had simply confronted Nicki about the guy she was cheating with. "The guy," based on Tim's timeline with the story, would have been Donovan, whom Nicki had been dating for four months at that point.

"It was my gun. My .380," Tim said.

"Was it loaded?" Officer Hook asked.

"My guns are always loaded," Tim responded. "And that's when I said, 'Before you pull that trigger, you might want to get Cal out of the room.'"

Tim claimed he then disarmed Nicki and "escorted her" out of his house.

"But you didn't call the cops in this particular incident? Just explain to me why," Officer Hook asked.

"That was just to a whole different-level crazy…" Tim began to say as he waved his hands around his head, thinking how to answer.

"Your priority was probably to just get out," Officer Hook finished answering for Tim.

Aspects of the story resembled the time Tim put a gun in his mouth with Cal in the room and threatened suicide. It almost seemed like Tim was trying to get ahead of Nicki in documenting the incident in a different way that could never be disproven if it came up in the custody case.

As for the foot incident, Tim claimed that when Nicki pulled her car forward after he slapped the hood, the vehicle struck Tim and knocked him to the ground. In reviewing the case, City

Attorney McClure looked at the surveillance video, which was filmed from the other side of the vehicle and partially obscured by a pillar, therefore not capturing where Tim's foot was located in relation to the tire. The camera angle also didn't capture whether the car physically touched Tim at all, but that's what McClure thought it showed.

Nicki can be seen in the video getting out of her SUV and following Tim into his gym. Tim told the officer that at that point, she was begging him not to call the police because she was worried she would lose her job. Tim told the officer he never called 911 during any of those incidents because Nicki would threaten to keep Callahan away from him.

After completing the police report, the officer left one voicemail on Nicki's phone and did not investigate further. The prosecutor filed the charge based on Tim's word, the obscured video, and no other corroboration. Nicki would have to fight the charges and earn an acquittal in order to preserve her career and—quite possibly—custody of her son.

CHAPTER THIRTEEN

The misdemeanor fifth-degree domestic assault trial was scheduled for January 10 at the Ramsey County Courthouse in Saint Paul. With Donovan there in the courtroom gallery for support, Nicki took her seat next to her attorney, Kelli Gaborsky, at the defendant's table as the jury trial began. The prosecutor, Luke McClure, called his first witness, Officer Nathan Hook, who testified that he was actively in training to become a detective.

Officer Hook gave a very basic overview of responding to Tim's call, watching the surveillance video, and determining if Nicki struck Tim with her car. Then, he left a voicemail for Nicki before forwarding his report to the prosecutor. In cross-examination, Kelli probed much further.

"Officer Hook, you didn't interview anyone except for Mr. Amacher. Is that correct?"

"Correct."

"So, did you get any other information, any corroborating evidence? Did you get any other corroborating witnesses or talk to anyone?" Kelli asked.

"No other physical witnesses," Officer Hook said.

When Officer Hook recorded Tim's statement in the Taekwondo studio office in August, a surveillance video monitor displaying views from nine different cameras was positioned right behind Tim. Kelli got the officer to admit that he never checked footage from any other camera angle. He didn't review the cameras inside the studio that would have captured Tim's interaction with Nicki immediately afterward and whether he continued to limp or display any sign of injury. The officer also failed to check the other cameras to see if another exterior angle provided a clear view of Tim's foot in relation to the SUV. In fact, Kelli got Officer Hook to acknowledge that he never even viewed a clear version of the video Tim presented to him. Instead, the evidence in the case was a low-quality cell phone recording of a video playing on a monitor—a video of a video. Kelli then raised further doubts about Officer Hook's investigation.

"Did Mr. Amacher tell you which foot was run over?" she asked.

"He stated he could not recall which one it was," Officer Hook said.

During his interview, Tim at first told the officer it was his right foot, then corrected himself to say it was his left foot before throwing up his hands and saying he couldn't remember. Despite the video showing the left side of Tim's body turned toward the SUV, the officer speculated in his testimony that, based on how Tim limped into the gym, Tim's right foot "may have been run over."

After a mid-morning break, McClure called Tim to the witness stand. As the only other witness in the prosecution's case, the jury would need to believe Tim's testimony to convict Nicki.

The fit Taekwondo master stood out in the courtroom wearing a shiny, tight, blue/gray custom-made suit and a pair of alligator skin cowboy boots. Tim began his testimony by giving the jury an overview of his work as a martial arts instructor and group fitness teacher, adding that he is trained in "verbal judo" to teach youth how to defend themselves with words.

Tim testified about his past relationship with Nicki, the birth of their son, and the arguments they had during parenting exchanges. Tim told the jury that he and Nicki dated all the way until August 8, 2018—which would have been more than a year into her relationship with Donovan and just one week before he called White Bear Lake Police to initiate the claims that brought them to court. If a witness lies during direct examination by a prosecutor, the defense can't object. They just file it away as something to revisit during cross-examination. Tim proceeded to lie about things very relevant to the accusations.

Judge Sophia Vuelo had granted McClure permission to question Tim about "past acts of domestic violence" he claimed were committed by Nicki. Judge Vuelo instructed the jury that Nicki wasn't being tried for anything other than the accusation involving her vehicle but that they could listen to the other stories to help inform their decision.

Tim claimed on the witness stand that sometime in 2015, Nicki had come after him with a knife.

"She was slashing and stabbing pictures of ours, and when I questioned her on why she was doing that, she then turned the knife on me," Tim testified.

In reality, at that time, late in their relationship, Nicki had discovered that Tim was sleeping with another woman. Nicki had just ordered a couple of canvas print photos of her and Tim that she was going to hang in their house, and—out of frustration upon learning of the affair—she destroyed the canvasses and threw them in the trash. Tim wasn't even home when she did it, but he belittled and berated her when he found the pictures in the trash. He apparently snapped a picture of the damaged canvas prints and held onto the photo to use against Nicki later.

McClure asked Tim about the Valentine's Day incident in Nicki's car. Tim gave his version in which he claimed Nicki attacked him inside and outside the vehicle.

"Sometimes she goes red," Tim testified. "I was afraid for my safety and my son's safety. More so, my son. I mean, things can happen to me, but I was more worried about him."

Finally, Tim told the jury his version of the incident outside his studio where he claimed Nicki ran over his foot, beginning with the argument that preceded it.

"As I approached the door to the studio, she leaned her head out the window and said something along the lines of, 'If you don't get *effing* back here, you'll never see your son again.' When I walked back to continue the conversation, that's when she rolled over my foot and then struck Callahan and myself with her vehicle," Tim said.

"She threatened you with never seeing your child again?" McClure asked.

"That's correct," Tim said.

"So, you went back to the vehicle. How close were you to her at that time?" McClure asked.

"Probably just like from me to the court reporter, maybe," Tim said, referring to the court employee seated near the witness stand typing a transcript of the testimony.

"So, a couple feet?" McClure asked.

"Yeah, close enough so the yelling wasn't necessary," Tim said.

Tim then testified that he couldn't remember what was said throughout the rest of the incident but that when Nicki pulled the car forward, it struck the side of his body while he was holding Callahan. McClure ended his direct examination by asking Tim why he waited three months and reported the incident in August after he had already decided to file custody papers. Tim had to know the question was coming, but he didn't seem prepared for it.

"Because of all of the threats that she had made and things that she's done, I can only see, with me standing up for my son and myself, that things would get a lot worse, and I wanted for people to know when things did get worse, I guess, is the best way to explain it. I just—I knew that things would get worse," Tim stammered.

After McClure finished his direct examination of Tim, the court broke for lunch. Upon returning, Tim started asking court personnel if he could meet with the judge alone. He wanted to make a complaint against Donovan, whom Tim claimed was glaring at him from the courtroom gallery and trying to intimidate him while he testified. Tim asked if Donovan could be removed from the courtroom.

The last time Tim and Donovan saw each other at a court hearing, Donovan sat in the hallway outside afterward with Rae. Tim walked out of the courtroom, unbuttoned his dress shirt, slung it over his shoulder, and walked past Donovan in his tank top undershirt, flexing his biceps.

"I guess that's supposed to intimidate me?" Donovan said to Rae as the two chuckled over Tim's absurd behavior.

This time, however, Tim's flex was getting the judge to remove Donovan from the proceedings on his behalf. When Kelli found out, she was furious. Nicki's parents were not able to attend the one-and-a-half-day trial because of unavoidable conflicts, and now Tim was trying to expel Nicki's lone loved one watching the trial.

"He's doing this because that's her one support person here. He's trying to alienate her and make her feel alone. He's playing games," Kelli said.

As a police officer, Donovan had experience testifying and certainly knew the finer points of courtroom decorum. He wouldn't do anything to jeopardize the proceedings. Nonetheless, Tim successfully influenced Judge Vuelo to ask Donovan to leave.

"I keep a close eye on everything going on in my courtroom, and I didn't see anything," Judge Vuelo said. "But in an abundance of cautiousness, to maintain a sense of neutrality and fairness to both the State and to Ms. Lenway, the court asked that this individual be removed immediately."

The incident only primed Kelli for her cross-examination. Her goal was to show the jury that Tim was a master manipulator and that—in this case—his manipulation of Officer Hook began with the very premise of Tim's call. Tim testified under direct examination that he had already filed for custody of Callahan and that he wanted advice from police on how to handle Nicki once she was served with the papers.

"You testified that you had filed your custody petition prior to the sixteenth, prior to that meeting, correct?" Kelli asked.

"I filed beforehand," Tim lied.

"Didn't you sign and file those documents when you were in Las Vegas on August 17? Isn't that true?" Kelli asked.

"That's correct, yes," Tim corrected himself.

"Being a master of Taekwondo, people call you 'Master,' correct?"

"Inside my facility, yes. Outside, no," Tim replied, unsure where Kelli was going with that line of questioning. Kelli knew the title fed Tim's ego. "Master" spoke not just to his martial arts expertise but to his self-image.

Kelli reminded Tim that part of the reasoning he gave for not reporting the alleged incidents sooner was that he is a man and that he worried people might not believe that a woman assaulted a man.

"That sounded like one of many reasons," Tim said.

"All right. What has changed, sir? You're still a man, correct?"

"That's correct."

"And you're also still a master of Taekwondo, correct?" Kelli asked.

"Correct."

"So, the only thing that's changed between then and now, sir, is the custody battle. Is that correct?" Kelli asked.

"There's a lot of things that have changed," Tim answered, irritated with the point Kelli successfully made.

Kelli pointed out several mischaracterizations Tim made concerning Nicki's job and her role within the police force. She didn't want the jury to believe Nicki used police connections to intimidate Tim. Then Kelli seized on the part of Tim's testimony that detailed his own expertise.

"I'm curious about 'verbal judo.' You stated in your testimony that you defend with words, correct?" Kelli asked.

"Correct."

"And so, are you a master at that as well?"

"Our school took a certification course to help educate kids on how to defend themselves against bullies," Tim said.

"So, do you know how to do verbal judo? Don't you practice it yourself?" Kelli asked, with her implication to the jury being that Tim was skilled with arguing and using his words to get what he wanted.

"I'm not hanging out with kids on playgrounds and getting bullied, so no," Tim answered.

"So even as an adult, people would not use verbal judo, only kids?" Kelli asked.

"Well, I prefer to walk away from situations," Tim answered.

"Uh-huh. OK," Kelli said in response, her sarcasm evident to each member of the jury.

Kelli then pivoted to the details of the allegation, pointing out that Tim had cameras inside the studio but did not show any of that video evidence to Officer Hook. At a prior court hearing, Tim had claimed to have photographs of his injured foot and bruised torso that he texted to Nicki. Tim said, somehow, that evidence had been deleted from both his phone and hers. Kelli made sure the jury remembered that Tim had never produced the "evidence" he had been talking about. Then, she began building up to the climax of her cross-examination.

"Did you go to the hospital?"

"No, I did not."

"Did you seek medical treatment?"

"No, I did not."

"Do you remember which foot it was?"

"No, I do not."

"Mr. McClure asked you how close you were. And you said you were a couple feet away from the vehicle. That was your testimony, correct?" Kelli asked.

"Yes," Tim answered.

Kelli had perfectly set up her gotcha question.

"If you were a couple feet away, how could she run over your foot?"

"She moved her car to get closer," Tim sputtered, realizing the gaping hole in his story that Kelli had just shown the jury.

"Really?" Kelli asked with an incredulous tone. "We watched the video, sir."

"She backed up. She backed up," Tim said as he started floundering on the witness stand.

"Uh-huh. She backed up slowly in the video," Kelli said.

"She backed…she looked like she moved her vehicle a few times," Tim stammered.

"Uh-huh," Kelli said.

As Tim continued to play into Kelli's hand, she began glancing at the jury, raising her eyebrows, and conveying a "get a load of this guy" subtext to them.

"We could re-watch the video, though, if you want," Tim suggested.

"Yeah, that'd be lovely," Kelli said as she brought the video back on the screen to show the jury how the images didn't match Tim's description. She then finished her cross-examination on that high note.

"You know, Mr. Amacher, I think that there's no further questions right now. Thank you," Kelli said.

CHAPTER FOURTEEN

In her job as a forensic scientist for the Minneapolis Police Department, Nicki had experience testifying in criminal trials. Those instances, however, involved explaining how she collected crime scene evidence. She had never been trained in how to testify on matters of the heart or matters involving her own child. In her own criminal trial, Nicki wanted to take the stand in her own defense. She was the final witness, the last person to present evidence to the jury before they heard closing arguments and deliberated her fate.

On the witness stand, Nicki gave the jury a brief history of her relationship with Tim, including how he continued trying to get back together with her after the custody filing and up to the month of the trial. Nicki went through various threats Tim made to ruin her career and to take her son by "doing whatever it took" to prove she was unfit as a mother.

Kelli asked Nicki to tell the jury what really happened in the two other allegations of domestic abuse Tim testified about—the canvas photo incident and the Valentine's Day car ordeal. Then, Kelli finished with the allegation that brought them all to court.

"Do you believe that you ran over Mr. Amacher's foot?" Kelli asked.

"No, I don't," Nicki said.

"Why do you believe that you didn't run over his foot?"

"He wasn't even injured. I have an SUV. And he had been threatening for months to try and use whatever he could against me. So that day, I immediately thought he was going to use this," Nicki said.

After Nicki's testimony, closing arguments began. Using a polished PowerPoint presentation with images from the surveillance video, McClure asked the jury to focus on intent, which is a required element to be proven beyond a reasonable doubt for both of Nicki's charges. McClure told them that the part on the video where Nicki pulled her SUV forward proved intent: She wanted to cause fear and harm to Tim. McClure emphasized that Nicki didn't apologize afterward.

Then, while touching on Nicki's testimony that Tim made up the allegations, the prosecutor unwittingly summed up the type of person Tim was and how far he was willing to go to get what he wanted.

"That would mean he planned ahead of time that he was going to fake his foot getting run over back in May and then, for some reason, wait, which really doesn't make sense. Why would he wait almost three months to call the police if he was going to fake this whole thing back in May?" McClure said. "Either Mr. Amacher is the type of man who premeditated this whole thing, staged it, faked his foot getting run over, and lied through his teeth today, or Ms. Lenway isn't being exactly honest with you about what happened that day."

When it was her turn to sum up the case, Kelli began by apologizing for not being as tech-savvy as McClure. She had no PowerPoint presentation, but she spent time locking eyes with each juror, one at a time, as she conversationally recounted the testimony and evidence from the trial.

Kelli acknowledged that Tim is a very charming and intelligent man. She pointed out that, as a master of Taekwondo, he is trained to fall to the ground the way he did on the video without hurting himself. Kelli asked the jury to use their common sense.

"Common sense is Ms. Lenway owns an SUV, a Nissan Rogue. That's almost two tons of car that allegedly ran over Mr. Amacher's foot, and he couldn't remember which foot! OK..." Kelli said, drawing out her last word for effect.

Kelli highlighted the cursory investigation conducted by Officer Hook: he interviewed no one else, he viewed no other camera angles, and he did nothing beyond taking Tim at his word. And Tim's word involved claims of additional evidence that never amounted to anything.

"He stated that he sent the photos to Ms. Lenway and that she deleted them. Well, doesn't he have copies? I mean, he has a video. Did he not show photos to the officer? If he was concerned that Ms. Lenway was going to do him harm, why would he send the photos to her? Why would he send evidence to her? I mean, was she going to take them to the police? So, where are the photos?" Kelli said.

As she wound down to the end of her closing argument, Kelli told the jury that even if they did believe Nicki ran over Tim's foot, she asked that they see it as an accident and nothing more. She highlighted the absurdity of the idea that Nicki would intentionally use her car as a weapon against Tim while he held her son. Kelli then finished by getting to the heart of the matter—the motive of Tim, the alleged victim, to make up the allegation.

"Because there is this custody situation coming up, I believe that sometimes, certain people will use what they can," she said. "Fighting over a child, I can't begin to imagine."

In trials such as these, the jury usually spends a half-day or longer to come to a unanimous verdict. Whether voting guilty or not guilty, all twelve of the jurors need to be in agreement before coming back into the courtroom. Even when strongly leaning in one direction, there most often are one or two jurors wanting to take a thorough look at the evidence before locking in their decision. Everyone in the courtroom was quite shocked when the bailiff walked in while the attorneys and judge were still finishing the legal process of putting information on the record.

"The jury's done," the bailiff said.

"They already have come up with a verdict?" Kelli asked.

While predicting verdicts can often be a fool's errand, quick verdicts generally tend to favor the prosecution. Yet, in this case, Kelli felt good about their chances. Nicki didn't know how to read into it. So much of her future—at work and with her son—rested on the jury's decision. Judge Vuelo began reading the verdict forms, one for each count of domestic assault.

"We, the jury, find the defendant not guilty of the charge of domestic assault, fear," Judge Vuelo read. "As to Count Two of the complaint, we, the jury, find the defendant not guilty of the charge of domestic assault, harm."

Nicki began crying tears of relief as she stood next to her attorney. Judge Vuelo offered her a tissue. Kelli began crying as well, looked at each person in the jury box, and thanked them individually.

"Ms. Lenway, I want to say congratulations to you," Judge Vuelo said, looking down from her bench with compassion. "I can't imagine the ordeal that you have been through. I also want to say good luck to you. You certainly have a lot on your plate, and I want to wish you the very best of luck as you continue to co-parent with the father of your child."

As they packed up their things and exited the courtroom, Nicki and Kelli ended up sharing an elevator with the prosecutor on their way out of the Ramsey County Courthouse. Kelli couldn't resist cracking a joke about Tim, the so-called victim that McClure hung his case on.

"You lost it when he wore those cowboy boots," she said, referring to Tim's flamboyant outfit.

The court victory lifted a huge weight from Nicki. Based on the lightning-quick verdict, lack of evidence against her, and the harm the allegation caused Nicki at work, Kelli filed a motion to expunge the case, which would seal all the records and remove the existence of the abuse charges from public view. Although it is rare for a judge to grant such a motion in cases that allege violence, even after a not-guilty verdict, the judge agreed to expunge the case against Nicki.

Nicki and Donovan both knew Tim would not take the loss in stride. The custody trial still loomed ahead. As the master manipulator grew more desperate, his accusations against both of them would only intensify.

CHAPTER FIFTEEN

In Minnesota family court, a judge is referred to as a referee. Referee Elizabeth Clysdale was assigned the custody case and combined the orders for protection requested by both Nicki and Tim, allowing her to manage all of the litigation together. Despite initially denying Tim's emergency request, after a trial, Referee Clysdale eventually issued an order for protection against both of them to prevent communication between Tim and Nicki.

As the two awaited Referee Clysdale's temporary custody plan, Nicki's parents helped watch Callahan while she worked. Forty days passed without Tim seeing Cal, prompting him to rally friends and acquaintances on his behalf. Next-door neighbor Charlie Dettloff received an invitation to meet at World Taekwondo Academy along with all the parents of Tim's Taekwondo students. Tim's lawyer was present, and they informed the group that Nicki was withholding Callahan from Tim and that he needed their support to vouch for him as a good parent and positive role model. None of the friends, clients, or acquaintances had conducted their own research on Tim's court claims. Having witnessed Tim's natural ease with their kids as their Taekwondo master and his interactions with Cal at the studio, most of them enthusiastically offered their help.

At least fifty of Tim's Taekwondo students and their family members signed a petition stating that, prior to the restraining order, Callahan was often present at World Taekwondo Academy and Underground Gym—also called Evolution Fitness Gym. Many of them wrote letters for Tim to submit to the court. While most were straightforward and supportive of Tim in the manner his lawyer suggested, some resorted to denigrating Nicki and her parenting.

"I have seen Nicki come in to drop off Cal. She looks very well put together while Cal does not—shirt is dirty, needs a diaper change, and is hungry," one woman wrote.

"I believe Ms. Lenway has been immature from the very beginning of their relationship, and I told Mr. Amacher this," another young woman wrote. "I knew it would be like this because I know Mr. Amacher. And Ms. Lenway was just not mature enough."

It hurt to read some of those words written by people who didn't even really know Nicki. However, the realization that Tim was able to influence so many people was even harder. When Referee Clysdale filed the temporary custody plan, she granted Nicki sole legal and physical custody with Tim essentially receiving two and a half days of parenting time every week. In addition, both parents would need to complete a custody evaluation with a licensed independent clinical social worker. The custody evaluator's report would be integral to Referee Clysdale's final decision at the custody trial. Tim and his lawyer objected to the professionals Nicki and her lawyer suggested for the evaluation. Finally,

Nicki agreed with Tim's preferred choice, Matthew Shore, who had more than ten years of experience as a mediator, parenting consultant, and custody evaluator.

With the custody trial still many months away, Tim began giving Nicki and Donovan more legal issues to contend with by filing reports with police and Child Protection Services (CPS). Tim's first report claimed that when he picked up Callahan for his parenting time, he noticed the boy had a swollen and bruised eye with makeup covering it up. He reported that Cal told him, "Mommy did it." After making the report to Saint Paul Police, Tim contacted Nicki's employer, the Minneapolis Police Department, and informed internal affairs, the office within MPD that investigates alleged employee misconduct.

One month after a jury found Nicki not guilty of domestic abuse, Tim contacted CPS and spoke to a supervisor. He wanted to report the same incident to them as well since he was holding Cal when he claimed Nicki ran over his foot and hit him with the car. Tim told CPS he believed the police were covering for Nicki.

While Tim's periodic police reports continued, he began taking Callahan to urgent care facilities during his parenting time despite not having legal and physical custody. As those doctor visits and reports began to mount in 2019, custody evaluator Matthew Shore began interviewing Tim and Nicki as part of the comprehensive court-ordered investigation. Throughout the year, Tim and Nicki both underwent required psychological evaluations. In the fall, Shore finally provided recommendations to the attorneys and issued his final report. The report provided a neutral analysis of Tim's behavior and revealed the effect it was having on Callahan.

During the interview process, Tim showed Mr. Shore a series of videos that Tim claimed were proof—in Callahan's own words—that Nicki and Donovan were hurting the boy. On the contrary, Shore wrote that Tim was coaching Cal on what to say in the videos.

"These interviews are deeply problematic. Cal is clearly being led in his answers, clearly does not appear to know what he is saying most of the time, is most frequently just repeating what his dad is telling him," Shore wrote.

Tim claimed that one of the videos proved that Cal was being instructed by Nicki to call Donovan "Daddy" instead of Tim. What Shore actually saw in the video was Tim confusing the young child by holding up photos and quizzing him.

"The videos are problematic in that they reflect leading and problematic influence over Cal that could lead to distortions and problems for him. Such interviewing must stop," Shore wrote.

While meeting with Shore, Tim told him the story of talking with Nicki's parents prior to Callahan's birth and asking for their blessing for him to propose. Tim told the evaluator that he recorded the conversation and that the Lenways reacted with racist statements. When Shore asked Tim to play the recording for him, Tim claimed he had deleted it at Nicki's request. That led Shore to believe the recording either never existed to begin with or didn't reveal what he claimed it did. Tim did show Shore the SUV versus Foot video, but Shore wrote that it did not match Tim's description.

Tim insisted that his police reports and doctor visits came in response to Nicki abusing Cal and that he responded as any caring father would. Shore made it clear that he did not believe Tim's claims, and Shore shared his analysis of what Tim was actually doing.

"I simply do not find the purported evidence of that allegation compelling. What I do see, however, is a possible manipulation of the facts by Tim to suit his needs and an overly focused lens that only allows him to view Nicole as abusive to Cal. This lens has, in turn, manifested itself in deeply inappropriate and leading interrogations of Cal that reveal a lack of understanding of developmental realities and a willingness to impose a narrative on matters that meets Tim's own needs more than Cal's," Shore wrote.

The psychological examinations provided Shore with some insight into Tim's personality and behavior. Dr. Jim Wojcik, a Minnesota psychologist, noted that Tim likely suffered "disrupted attachment and a hardening of his personality" stemming from his father's suicide and abuse that Tim suffered at the hands of his mother when he was a child. Tim's childhood abuse and abandonment, according to the psychologist, led to coping mechanisms rooted in defense and self-preservation as an adult.

"Stresses such as these may result in rationalization behaviors such as taking advantage of others, dishonesty, or projection of blame," Dr. Wojcik wrote. "At the same time, Mr. Amacher presents himself as virtuous."

The psychological assessment cast doubt on Tim's prospects of successfully co-parenting with Nicki.

"These behaviors and personality features suggest a high degree of difficulty for his co-parent as she attempts to function, as he may regularly make accusations of her character or offer explanations of his behavior that are inaccurate," Dr. Wojcik wrote. "In a further and more important issue, Mr. Amacher demonstrates the potential model of antisocial attitudes for his son. This includes fabrication of information or lying."

Shore agreed with Dr. Wojcik's findings in the psychological assessment and ultimately recommended that Tim receive less parenting time than he was currently entitled to under Referee Clysdale's temporary order. In fact, Shore recommended that Tim's parenting time only come under supervision.

"I believe, as a consequence, in this context, that Tim's parenting time should be restricted until he can show himself better able to contemplate Nicole as something other than a threat," Shore wrote.

The custody trial itself was still months away, giving Tim ample time to take the custody evaluation recommendations to heart and change his behavior. Instead, Tim would go on to make an additional fifteen reports to doctors, police, and CPS. And Tim's accusations only grew more demented.

CHAPTER SIXTEEN

Thanksgiving 2019 was a wonderful celebration with Nicki's extended family at her parents' home. Nicki's parents, grandparents, cousins, aunts, and uncles were there, along with Nicki, Donovan, and Callahan. The following Monday, however, Nicki received a call from a Burnsville police detective asking for Donovan's contact information. Tim had reported to them that Donovan sexually abused Callahan.

"Boyfriend pinched my penis," Tim claimed Cal told him when he picked up the child on Sunday at the end of the holiday weekend.

The accusation shook Donovan. By that point, he had already testified on Nicki's behalf at the order for protection trial and supported her in court during the domestic assault trial. He had received threatening calls and texts from Tim. Now, while on the phone with a detective from the Burnsville Police Department investigating a claim of sexual abuse, the possibility of losing his career, family, and freedom due to Tim's lies loomed large.

Tim claimed the incident happened on Thanksgiving when Donovan and Cal were alone after the meal. Thankfully, as several of Nicki's family members could corroborate, Donovan and Cal were never alone at the Lenway house that day. When Nicki left for work that night, Donovan left as well to go early-Black Friday shopping. He provided receipts to the detective, allowing the police to close the case as an unfounded claim.

The effect of the sexual abuse claim continued to resonate. Nicki and Tim had started using FamilyWise Services to facilitate parenting exchanges so that they did not need to come face to face. Unaware of Tim's coaching of Callahan, a FamilyWise staff member got concerned while hearing Cal repeat portions of the disturbing allegation and reported it to CPS. Donovan knew the report would reach internal affairs at the Minneapolis Police Department, so he preemptively addressed it with his supervisors. Nicki was absolutely furious that Tim would stoop to that level, but as she and Donovan began to think about it with clear heads, they weren't surprised. They saw Tim's escalation as the next twisted step for someone who was willing to do anything to get what he wanted.

"We don't know what he's going to report or when, so I don't think I should spend time around Cal until the custody trial is over," Donovan told Nicki, as they agreed to avoid situations without other people present who could corroborate Donovan's innocence.

It was fortunate that they devised that plan. A few months later, Tim contacted the Saint Paul Police to report burns on Callahan's fingers. Tim informed the officer that when he asked his son how it happened, the three-year-old responded, "Boyfriend fire," and "Boyfriend bad man." As it turned out,

Callahan had accidentally touched the wood-burning stove at Nicki's grandparents' house, which resulted in blisters forming on his fingertips. Nicki called the nurse's line at Cal's pediatrician that day, and they advised her to ice it, monitor for infection, and give him ibuprofen if pain relief seemed necessary.

Tim began to deploy his live-in student, Colleen, to help him document a case against Nicki and Donovan to use at the custody trial. Colleen handled a lot of the parenting exchanges at FamilyWise on Tim's behalf, and she served as Cal's nanny for Tim either at home or the Taekwondo studio while Tim taught classes.

In his next police report, Tim claimed that when Colleen began emptying Callahan's bag in front of Tim, she found a live nine millimeter hollow point bullet, which Cal said came "from Mama's house." Tim told police there had been "many different incidents of harassment and intimidation" by Nicole and Donovan. He even exaggerated his own previous lie from the domestic abuse trial, telling police Donovan made gestures of "cocking a gun" toward him from the courtroom gallery, forcing the judge to address it. Tim told police the bullets seemed to show Donovan was trying to "intimidate him again."

Before Tim's escalation of false reports, Donovan and Nicki's relationship had reached a stage where, under normal circumstances, moving in together would have made sense. They even discussed marriage. However, due to the chaos Tim was creating in their lives, they settled into a holding pattern. With two children of his own and sharing custody equally with his ex-wife, Donovan wanted to do everything possible to shield them from the drama and potential danger. Worst of all, discontent in the relationship was just what Tim was attempting to create.

At least another four times that year, Donovan had to sit down with police detectives or social workers to defend himself, humiliated by the content of the allegations. He was stressed by the continued need to restart his story from the beginning, rehashing his alibis and emphasizing that nothing Tim reported was accurate. Each time Tim leveled a new claim, Donovan immediately informed his MPD supervisors, which automatically triggered an internal affairs review. He made it clear he wasn't trying to hide anything.

When the volume and frequency of false reports peaked, with Tim even approaching Donovan's coworkers to spread the lies, Nicki's criminal defense lawyer, Kelli Gaborsky, drafted a cease-and-desist letter and sent it to Tim on Donovan's behalf.

"That is crime, Mr. Amacher. It is not clear what you hope to gain by this harassing behavior. To be clear, this letter is notice that if you continue stating fabrications, lies, and defamations regarding Officer Ford, legal action will be taken against you, and this matter will be resolved in the courts," Kelli wrote.

In March 2020, the world changed with the onset of the COVID-19 pandemic. Two months later, Minneapolis became the epicenter of widespread social unrest after the death of George Floyd. As riots commenced, and the city burned, Donovan spent days saving fellow first responders and trying to stop arsonists and looters. Public sentiment toward the Minneapolis Police Department reached an all-time low.

Although he had his kids, Nicki, and her family in Minnesota, the climate in Minneapolis began to make Donovan feel isolated. He missed his own family in Colorado and wanted his children to be near them during that difficult time. Believing it would also offer a fresh start from the ongoing baseless allegations made by Tim, Donovan made the tough decision to move back to Colorado. Nicki talked about relocating there with him, but she knew it wouldn't be feasible with the ongoing custody battle still pending.

Nicki had always been a believer in fate, that things would work out the way they were supposed to. With that, she agreed that Donovan needed to do what was best for him and his children. He applied for a police job in Colorado and resigned from his position with the Minneapolis Police Department in good standing. The couple transitioned to a long-distance relationship in October 2020, visiting each other periodically and trying to make it all work. The long-awaited custody trial loomed ahead, just one month away.

CHAPTER SEVENTEEN

As Nicki and her family court attorney, Stacy Lofgren, prepared for the custody trial, they started pulling all the police reports Tim had filed. Nicki hadn't known until then that Tim was bringing Callahan to urgent care appointments without her knowledge. They requested the medical records from the facilities where Tim took Cal. Those doctor notes, along with police officer notes on the corresponding reports, revealed a number of lies Tim had told while trying to build his case.

Within days of Referee Clysdale filing the initial custody order in late 2018, Tim reported to Saint Paul Police that Nicki had "violated the court order five times in the past two weeks." That lie resulted in police notifying the social services departments in both Ramsey and Hennepin Counties and initiating CPS investigations on the unfounded claims.

In another report, separate from the Thanksgiving sexual abuse claim, Tim told Saint Paul Police that Callahan had a laceration on his penis. The officer wrote in his report that Tim started crying while telling him that he was afraid to report abuse because of the threats coming from Nicki and Donovan due to their jobs with the Minneapolis Police Department. Tim misrepresented Nicki's job as well, telling police that she was an officer with MPD.

In the report regarding the bullet Tim claimed Colleen found in Callahan's bag, Tim told police that Colleen was a worker at FamilyWise. He told that officer about his prior claim of Nicki running over his foot, but he described it as if he and Cal were "struck down by Nicki." Tim lied about the jury acquittal, claiming the case was dropped when he tried to prosecute Nicki.

At least once, Tim told police that Nicki was his ex-wife and that the couple shared custody. Tim, in fact, never had custody; the referee's temporary order had only provided him with unsupervised parenting time. When asked by one doctor why Tim wasn't bringing Cal to his primary care physician, Tim lied and said Nicki worked at that clinic. He claimed he couldn't bring Cal there with injuries caused by Nicki because of the conflict of interest and the likelihood she would find out and nothing would be done.

All those discrepancies provided Nicki's attorney with plenty of material to use at the trial. In addition, Matthew Shore's custody evaluation report, which recommended Tim's parenting time be reduced strictly to supervised visits, would carry a lot of weight with the judge. After multiple delays due to COVID-19, when the trial finally commenced at the Ramsey County Courthouse in November 2020, Tim's attorney got to present their case first, since he was the petitioner who initiated the legal action.

Tim took the witness stand to be questioned by his attorney, Margaret Westin. He described himself as a devoted, hands-on father, painting a glowing picture of his parenting practices before shifting to anecdotes about Nicki allegedly alienating Cal, now four years old, from him.

"I said, 'What's the matter, buddy? I missed you so much. I love you.' He said, 'You don't miss me. You don't love me. You hate me.' That was the first time I ever heard the word 'hate' come out of his mouth. And I just explained to him, I said, 'Daddy doesn't hate you. Daddy loves you. Daddy did miss you.' Cal said, 'Mama said that you hate me. Mama said that you don't miss me,'" Tim testified.

Margaret then asked Tim to go through each abuse claim that he documented in his journal after filing custody paperwork. As Tim told his version of those stories, Margaret put corresponding photos on the screen. In some of the pictures, light bruising could be seen, but nothing more than what any rambunctious young boy might get from ordinary play.

"What did your son tell you at that time?" Margaret asked about one of the photos that Tim insisted showed a bump on Callahan's head.

"He said, 'Mama house. Mama house. Mama go boom!' And he made sort of a fist motion toward his head," Tim said.

Tim testified that after finding bruising on Cal's back, he recorded multiple videos of Cal answering Tim's questions about what had happened. That testimony went right to the heart of custody evaluator Matthew Shore's concerns about Tim confusing the child, coaching him, and then recording out-of-context videos to document the narrative Tim wanted to present.

"In all my career in Taekwondo, even when I was competing on a combat level, you just don't get injuries like these. I mean, A: I believe what my son says; B: a lot of these injuries are similar to stuff that Nicole has done to me in the past," Tim said, adding allegations of domestic abuse from Nicki to his testimony. Tim even claimed Nicki stomped on her son's foot with her high-heeled shoe.

Tim proceeded into his allegations of sexual abuse against Donovan and Nicki, claiming Cal told him that even Nicki once twisted the boy's penis to hurt him. From there, Tim began telling a bizarre story, accusing Donovan of torturing Cal with an electric drill.

"We were getting ready to go outside and play, and he started freaking out when I was getting ready to put on his shoes. He started making like a 'Zzz, zzz,' like a drilling sound," Tim testified. "So then I looked at his shoe and noticed that his shoe had a marking, once again, that I have never seen before on a shoe, and it looks like a drill mark."

When Tim's laborious, self-serving testimony involving abuse allegations finally ended, Margaret asked him for his opinion on the court's ultimate custody decision. Tim said he wanted Nicki to undergo court-ordered anger management courses before she is allowed to see her son unsupervised.

"After someone signs off on saying that she's safe to be around, I'd be willing to revisit the courts and say she can have fifty/fifty," Tim said. "But right now, I fear for his well-being on all levels—mental, physical."

CHAPTER EIGHTEEN

Nicki's attorney, Stacy Lofgren, in cross-examination, began to use Tim's testimony against him. Several of his allegations of child abuse, in which he admitted to interviewing and video recording Callahan, came after Tim received the custody evaluation report and recommendations. Those recommendations, one year prior to the trial, warned him to stop.

"Are you aware of the concern that Matthew Shore articulated about the videos and the interviewing you were doing with Callahan? You're aware that he wrote that in his report, yes or no?"

"Yes," Tim said.

"And you're aware of the recommendation he made, indicating that supervised parenting time for you may be appropriate if those allegations continued to be made. Are you aware of that recommendation?" Stacy asked.

"Correct," Tim said.

Stacy went through the numerous police reports filed by Tim, pointing out discrepancies, misrepresentations, and lies. Tim admitted bringing Callahan to the Midwest Children's Resource Center, the arm of Children's Hospital Minnesota that handles child abuse claims. Callahan was interviewed on camera at those visits, and in one report from Saint Paul Police, they noted the MCRC was no longer willing to see Tim after they could find no domestic abuse, and they believed the visits were doing Callahan more harm than good.

Tim admitted under cross-examination that he proactively made reports to Minneapolis Police internal affairs at least twice, secretly recording his conversations with internal affairs investigators. By filing the reports at Minneapolis City Hall downtown in the same building where Nicki worked, Tim would be in violation of the order for protection against him.

"So, in filing a report against Ms. Lenway, were you trying to jeopardize her employment in some fashion?" Stacy asked.

"No, I could…she can…no. I'm…" Tim stammered. "I filed reports because reports need to be filed. If somebody does something wrong, if my son is telling me he's being abused, then I'm going to advocate for my son."

"OK. And Ms. Lenway has an order for protection against you that was in effect at that time that prohibits you from going to the city hall building, correct?" Stacy asked.

"I don't believe that is correct," Tim answered at first, before finally agreeing with Stacy after she showed him the OFP document.

After listening to testimony about Tim secretly recording various conversations and interviews, Referee Clysdale grew suspicious about a black box Tim had set in front of him on the witness stand. She asked him what it was, and Tim told her it was a Bluetooth speaker he brought along in case he needed to play videos from his phone. Referee Clysdale examined the device to ensure it had no record function, which would have violated courtroom rules, before she allowed Stacy's cross-examination to continue.

Tim was defiant when Stacy showed him that none of the reports he filed, with the exception of the SUV versus Foot allegation, resulted in any charges or findings of abuse. Tim insisted he was still awaiting follow-up phone calls from authorities. Stacy read reports aloud to Tim as he followed along with printed copies that plainly stated the cases were closed.

"Based on the totality of the circumstances, I am not able to substantiate that any abuse has or had occurred," Stacy read. "Do you see that?"

"Yes," Tim answered.

She showed him another report.

"'I don't believe there is evidence to support the burns on Callahan's fingers to have been caused intentionally.' Do you see that determination? And under 'status,' the report indicates 'unfounded.'" Stacy pointed out.

"Yes, I see that's what is written on this sheet of paper," Tim responded.

Stacy pulled up yet another report.

"It looks like the determination of this police department as well was that no crime was committed, and there would be no further investigation. Do you see that?" Stacy asked.

"Yes, I see where it says that," Tim said.

Regarding the doctor visits, Tim said the reason he didn't take Cal to the primary care physician was that Nicki and Rae "verbally attacked" him when they were there days after he filed the custody petition and that he "did not feel safe at that clinic."

"And so you unilaterally decided to take him to a different clinic?" Stacy asked.

"That is correct," Tim said.

"And then this report goes on to say, 'Father informs me that patient's mother is an employee at the clinic.' Obviously, you knew that Ms. Lenway was not an employee of the Allina Bandana Clinic, correct?" Stacy asked.

"I never said that," Tim responded.

"So, this report is inaccurate?" Stacy asked.

"No. Like I said, there are parts of it that are accurate, and there are parts that are inaccurate," Tim said.

"Then, toward the middle of the page, the doctor writes, 'Father not happy with future plans,'" Stacy read.

"I don't even know what that means," Tim responded.

"Were you dissatisfied with the conclusions drawn or not drawn by the physicians that day?" Stacy asked.

"No," Tim insisted.

After Tim finished more than a day of testimony, other witnesses began to testify in the custody trial. Stacy called Julie Finnerty, a Dakota County social worker who investigated two of Tim's claims. Her interviews with Callahan proved Tim was coaching the young boy and drawing out answers Tim wanted with leading questions. Julie's testimony helped begin to expose the truth.

"It looks like you asked Callahan about the mark on his foot?" Stacy asked.

"Yes. Callahan told me, 'Daddy said Mommy did it,'" Julie responded.

"And you proceeded to ask him again, correct? What did he say the next time?" Stacy asked.

"That he did not know what happened," Julie said.

"Then he went on without you asking another question. What did he say to you?" Stacy asked.

"He said, 'Daddy will say that Donovan hurts me, and I will tell him he does not hurt me,'" Julie said.

"And then he also said, 'Mommy does not hurt me, and Daddy does not hurt me?'" Stacy asked.

"Correct," Julie testified.

Tim's attorney called a few other witnesses, including Colleen. Nicki knew Colleen spent time with Cal; she had picked him up sixty-five times on Tim's behalf at the parenting swaps at FamilyWise and was Tim's go-to babysitter and nanny. During Colleen's testimony, however, Nicki was surprised by how involved she had been in helping Tim document things to use in the trial.

Similar to Tim's testimony, Colleen went through a list of documented observations she claimed could have stemmed from abuse as Tim's attorney cycled through photographs Colleen took of the boy. Some days, Colleen spent a lot of time with Cal before Tim saw the child. Stacy raised the possibility that if Tim did find any legitimate marks, they could have happened while Cal was in Colleen's care.

Finally, when Nicki took the stand, she credibly refuted every claim made by Tim. She testified about her parenting and the loving home she provides for Callahan along with the support she receives from her parents and extended family. Stacy then asked Nicki about the end of her relationship with Tim.

"Has Mr. Amacher ever threatened you regarding not wanting to stay together?" Stacy asked.

"Yes," Nicki said.

"And what type of threats were made?" Stacy asked.

"He told me that he would try to take Callahan away from me, he would take away my livelihood by taking away my job, and that he would inundate me with court fees to the point where I would be broke, and my parents would be broke," Nicki testified.

At the end of the four-day trial, Stacy left Referee Clysdale with the parting message that the entire custody case was brought on by Tim as retaliation for Nicki's rejection of him. In her written closing argument, Stacy extensively cited the custody evaluation done by Matthew Shore—the evaluator Tim's attorney recommended—and asked Referee Clysdale to adopt his recommendation to limit Tim to supervised contact with Cal.

"Since the parties' relationship ended, Mr. Amacher was and is still unable to accept the fact Ms. Lenway does not want to be in a relationship with him. Since the day Ms. Lenway made that fact known, Mr. Amacher has made it nearly a singular mission to ruin her life."

CHAPTER NINETEEN

On Christmas Eve 2020, one month after the end of the custody trial, Referee Elizabeth Clysdale had still not issued her decision. Nicki was at home, getting ready to pick up Callahan at FamilyWise after his visit with Tim. As they awaited the decision, Nicki was forced to resume the parenting exchanges as set up in the previous temporary custody order. Each exchange made Nicki more nervous, as it was clear to everyone in the courtroom that the trial had not gone well for Tim, and the result was unlikely to be in his favor.

What would he try next? Nicki wondered.

At about 4:45 p.m., the doorbell at Nicki's house rang.

"Can I help you?" Nicki asked the woman standing at her doorstep.

The woman introduced herself as Theresa Roberts, a Dakota County Child Protection social worker. She was irritated, telling Nicki she was forced to respond to Nicki's home in person because Nicki hadn't returned any of her calls.

"You can look at my phone. I have no missed calls from you and no voicemails," Nicki explained, dreading what Theresa was going to share next.

"Because you didn't respond to me, here's what's happening," Theresa said. "Tim has filed a report. I believe Tim, and I believe Callahan. He is in danger, and he is scared of you, so he won't be coming back here. And I'll be recommending he doesn't."

"Is there anybody I can talk to? Tim's doing this because it's Christmas. Now he'll have Cal through the holidays. Who can change this?" Nicki desperately asked.

"My day ends now," Theresa said, referencing the time nearing 5:00 p.m., the close of business on Christmas Eve. "You won't be able to get ahold of anybody until after the holiday."

"Do you know any of the history in this case?" Nicki asked, flabbergasted that anyone who took even a cursory look at Tim's prior behavior would believe him.

"Tim has made it pretty clear that everything has been biased toward him. He's not getting a fair shake. Because of that, I'm going to take this report for what it is," Theresa said.

"Then you're not getting the whole story. We have a very extensive history!" Nicki said.

"Oh, I know!" Theresa said, her voice rising as well. "You're white and work in law enforcement. Tim is Black, and the system is just not listening to him. No one is listening to him. It's understandable with everything that happened to George Floyd and you working for MPD that he would feel this way," said Theresa, who was Black herself.

"That's super offensive and inappropriate. I have nothing to do with any of that. I'm a civilian employee, not a cop," Nicki responded.

Nicki was stunned. Tim had found someone who believed his lies at face value, and this woman had the power to separate a mother and son on their most important holiday. Every year since Cal was born, they spent Christmas Eve at Nicki's parents' house. They would wake up on Christmas morning, and Cal would open presents under the tree. Now, at four and a half, Cal was at the perfect age for believing in Christmas magic, and that fleeting, irreplaceable moment was being stolen from them.

Tim set the events in motion earlier that afternoon by calling Dakota County Child Protection, which sent Theresa to his house. At about 3:30 p.m., Theresa called Saint Paul Police. She told the arriving officer that Dakota County Child Protection would be taking custody of Callahan and placing him with Tim for seventy-two hours. Tim had convinced Theresa that Nicki threw a stick at Callahan and that the boy was afraid to go home with her. To help convince her of his story, Tim had told Theresa that a hospital had documentation of bruises on Cal's body. When Theresa asked the boy who had hurt him, he answered that his mom had. Having not reviewed any of the case history, Theresa did not know about Tim's habit of coaching his son to say what he wants. When police arrived at Tim's home, the boy was in a deep sleep, and they could not wake him.

Before Theresa left Nicki's house, the two determined Theresa had been dialing the wrong area code when trying to reach Nicki.

Was that Theresa's mistake, or had Tim intentionally given her the wrong number? Regardless, Theresa told Nicki there was nothing she could do besides go to court after the holiday and see what a judge would decide. After delivering that news, Theresa was gone, and Nicki felt very alone.

Nicki called her parents and her attorney, then started calling every county service and local police department she could think of to try and figure out exactly what was happening and how she could get Cal back. But Theresa was right. No one was answering the phone after business hours on Christmas Eve. With Christmas Day falling on a Friday, that meant Nicki had very few options until Monday, December 28.

How is this even possible? How is this happening? Nicki wondered.

What was supposed to be a comforting, long holiday weekend with Callahan and her family became a waking nightmare. Nicki felt like a zombie—numb, violated, and helpless. The one olive branch extended by Theresa before she left Nicki's house was that she agreed to facilitate a call between Nicki and Tim so that Nicki could talk with her son on Christmas. When that time came, however, Tim would not create a distraction-free environment for Callahan to take the FaceTime video call.

"Cal doesn't want to come to the phone. He's too busy doing stuff with his presents. Maybe you can try back later," Tim said, rushing Nicki off the call.

Nicki texted Tim directly three hours later, asking what time would work best to call back. Tim responded, "When Cal got up from his nap, I asked him if he wanted to talk with you again. Cal said no." After that, Tim ceased communication.

When Monday, December 28, finally came, Nicki's lawyer, Stacy Lofgren, spoke with Theresa Roberts by phone and learned more details of Tim's claim. Stacy asked Theresa if she had read through prior CPS reports before making her decision, and Theresa sidestepped the question. The social worker said she based her decision on her interview with Cal along with a video Tim provided her. When Stacy asked why Theresa didn't talk with Nicki before making a decision, Theresa cut her off.

"This feels like an inquisition. This can all wait until the court hearing on Wednesday," Theresa said.

Before ending the call, Theresa added that she had a substantiated report that Nicki tried to "run them over with a car," referring to the expunged assault case from White Bear Lake.

"That is not what that report says," Stacy said. "Why would you base your decision on that report but disregard more recent unfounded reports Tim made to your own Child Protection office?"

Theresa had no response. Two days later, on December 30, the court hearing Theresa had alluded to was still not scheduled to address the incident with a judge. The seventy-two-hour hold initiated by Theresa had expired. Callahan was returned to Nicki a full seven days after she had last seen him. When she brought him to her parents' home that day, what Callahan told them was extremely upsetting.

"Daddy says you all hate me. You don't want me, and that's why you didn't come and get me," Callahan said to his heartbroken mother and grandparents.

CHAPTER TWENTY

After finally finding someone who believed his claims, Tim took full advantage. He continued making reports to Theresa Roberts as the sides continued waiting for the custody ruling. In March 2021, Tim claimed Callahan woke up at his house and told him Nicki and Donovan both fondled him and that he was afraid Donovan would crawl through the window and hurt him.

Theresa drove to Tim's house and interviewed Cal again with Tim in the home. She asked the child questions about those claims as well as new accusations Tim made the previous week that Nicki had "punched and smacked" Cal. Tim told Theresa that Donovan was a "sexual predator" and that Nicki engaged in sexual abuse herself. Theresa told Tim she would schedule a home visit with Nicki. And that's when the allegation blew up in Tim and Theresa's faces.

Tim apparently was unaware that Donovan had moved back to Colorado four months earlier in November. Donovan had not been back to Minnesota to visit since then. There was no way he could have done the things Tim claimed he was doing. Nicki was appalled yet not completely surprised that Theresa continued to maintain her belief in Tim.

"Did Donovan visit Callahan at some time?" Theresa kept asking Nicki during follow-up Zoom meetings. Theresa assigned another social worker to visit Nicki and Cal weekly at Nicki's house to check up on them. Tim tried using that botched allegation to obtain an order for protection to take Cal from Nicki, but a judge declined to sign it.

After the latest incident involving clear coaching from Tim telling Callahan what to say to Theresa and other authorities, Nicki's mom, Rae, talked with Cal. Approaching his fifth birthday in just a few months, Cal was able to articulate his thoughts much better than when Tim's coaching began. Rae asked him why he would say that his mom was hurting him.

"Cuz Daddy says to," Cal responded.

"You should always tell the truth," Rae responded. "Do you know what the truth is?"

"No, I'm confused," Cal said.

"The truth is what really happens. Not just what someone says happens," Rae explained.

"Daddy would get mad if I didn't say it, and Daddy is mean when he's mad," Cal said.

That wasn't the only conversation that concerned Rae. One night, while she was watching the boy, Rae put him to bed and said prayers with him. She noticed that Callahan said a prayer for Mommy.

"That was nice of you to pray for Mommy," Rae told him.

"Daddy says we have to pray for Mommy because we are going to Heaven, and Mommy isn't," Callahan said.

Over the following days, a different social worker from Dakota County reached out to Nicki and said a forensic interview with Cal was needed because of the sexual nature of the newest allegations. A Burnsville Police detective, along with a social worker trained in such interviews, would be asking questions.

Nicki was not allowed to watch the interview. When social worker Jennifer Dockter came out of the room afterward, she reassured Nicki that Callahan told them his mom never hurt him. The boy did say, however, that his dad had gotten mad and hurt him before. Jennifer said she had no doubt Cal was safe with Nicki, but she expressed serious doubts about Cal's safety with Tim. Nicki told Jennifer and the Burnsville detective about her prior meetings with Theresa. They agreed with Nicki that Theresa was not handling the clearly unfounded case properly.

The following few weeks brought a series of good news to Nicki. She received a voicemail and letter from Theresa confirming she was dropping her investigation of Tim's Christmas Eve claims. A judge signed an emergency order for protection keeping Cal from Tim based on concerns stemming from the forensic interview. Jennifer sent Nicki a letter informing her that Dakota County Social Services was dropping the subsequent sexual abuse investigation stemming from the report when Donovan was gone. And finally, Referee Clysdale issued her long-awaited custody decision stemming from the trial and proceedings initiated by Tim.

Referee Clysdale granted Nicki sole legal and physical custody of Callahan. She limited Tim's parenting time to supervised visits once per week for up to two hours at FamilyWise. Tim would be strictly prohibited from asking Cal about perceived or actual injuries. After taking three parenting coaching sessions, Tim would have to continue supervised parenting sessions for six months without making any false accusations of physical or sexual abuse. If he reached those benchmarks, Referee Clysdale would reinstate Tim's unsupervised parenting time two nights a week. Nicki would have Cal every holiday except for Father's Day and Tim's birthday.

Referee Clysdale's validation was also very important to Nicki. Throughout the twenty-eight-page written ruling, the judge noted how Tim sought to undermine Nicki and manipulate situations to his advantage. Regarding anything Cal might have said to authorities that supported Tim's claims, Referee Clysdale wrote, "It is very likely that during Father's interviews and recording of the child, the child would say whatever Father wants him to say in order to please him and gain his approval."

Referee Clysdale extensively cited the findings in Matthew Shores's neutral custody evaluation, noting that Tim's attorney recommended using Shore. The custody evaluator opined that the "mayhem and difficulty (caused by Tim) must end, or Cal will remain at real risk moving forward." The judge agreed, writing that Tim's behavior put Cal's emotional development at risk, likely causing him to question his ability to know who to trust.

"Father is conditioning the child to believe he is being hurt by Mother and Mr. Ford, which is extremely unhealthy for the child and will result in emotional endangerment if it has not already," Referee Clysdale wrote.

The judge noted how Tim's legal actions appeared retaliatory toward Nicki. Whereas Nicki only asked to limit Tim's parenting time after he started filing the false reports.

"The benefit of Father's unsupervised parenting time with the child is being outweighed by Father's emotional harm the Father is causing the child while the child is in his care," Referee

Clysdale wrote. "Until Father can stop making false allegations against Mother and those aligned with her and appropriately support Mother's relationship with the child, Father's parenting time should be supervised."

Testimony at the trial itself affected the judge's decision. Referee Clysdale noted all the lies Tim told police and medical professionals and how his testimony to the contrary lacked credibility. She noted the differences in body language between Tim and Nicki during the trial. When Tim talked about Cal from the witness stand, Nicki smiled and appeared to agree with Tim's descriptions of Cal. When Nicki spoke, Referee Clysdale noticed Tim appeared angry and clenched and unclenched his fists.

With Tim's parenting time restricted, the unfounded reports finally stopped. Nicki felt safer. She hoped it would last.

CHAPTER TWENTY-ONE

Supervised visits at FamilyWise began in June 2021. The rules required Tim to arrive first, park in a separate lot, and then get into place in the visitation room before Nicki arrived with Callahan. At the end of a visit, Nicki was required to arrive at the front door neither early nor late to pick up Cal from a staff member. They would then release Tim fifteen minutes later so that he and Nicki would not cross paths while leaving the facility.

The FamilyWise staff member supervising each visit took notes of her observations, including what Tim and Cal would say to each other. At the end of each month, the facility would provide copies of the notes to Nicki's attorney. It didn't take long for Nicki to find several concerning things within those notes.

The court order laid out in great detail Tim's use of secret recordings to manipulate situations, plus his regular recording and interrogation of Callahan. Despite FamilyWise rules stating that electronic devices must be off during visits to prevent recording, the notes—right from the first visit—revealed Tim was using his phone.

Tim was able to talk the supervisor into letting him play music from his phone to a Bluetooth speaker during his visit. The supervisor also allowed Tim to use an app to teach Cal Spanish vocabulary. Those ideas sounded harmless and even beneficial to improving the father-son relationship, as is FamilyWise's goal, but those staff members had no idea how skilled Tim was in the art of manipulation. They didn't appreciate the warning Nicki and her lawyer gave regarding what Tim might try if allowed to use his phone during visits.

As soon as Nicki began raising concerns with Glorina Fruetel, FamilyWise's supervised parenting manager, she felt resistance. While Glorina acknowledged that the center didn't follow its own rules regarding electronic devices, she defended what had occurred because she believed they were fostering a positive environment. Nicki pointed out several other issues that were documented in the notes.

During visits, Tim was not supposed to comment on Nicki's parenting. Yet, Nicki read that a supervisor noted when Tim asked Cal whether Nicki took him to church and prayed with him. The topic of praying had already stuck with Nicki because disturbing references to going to Heaven "soon…without Mommy" had already come up during bedtime prayers at home. After Nicki pointed out to FamilyWise that Tim wasn't supposed to ask Cal about her parenting, the visit notes reflected that Tim twisted it back around, telling Cal, "We can't pray together anymore."

For multiple reasons, including the possibility of parental abduction, the supervised visits were supposed to take place inside the FamilyWise facility. However, the notes reflected times that Tim and Cal would go for a walk outside to a nearby park, concerning Nicki that the supervisor following them would not be able to hear the things Tim was telling the boy.

At some of the initial visits, Cal repeated to his dad some of the unfounded claims Tim had coached him to make, such as "Mama hit me with a stick." The boy no doubt remembered the positive reinforcement his dad would give him during the custody battle if he repeated such things. When Cal repeated those allegations during a visit, Tim looked to the supervisor with a defeated expression. He said, "I don't know how I'm supposed to respond to that," eliciting sympathy from FamilyWise staff.

Tim was finding clever ways to gaslight the FamilyWise workers without them believing he was violating the rules or the court order. Nicki worried that Tim was further turning them against her. He told workers that Callahan had arrived to visits with bullets and a knife in his bag—a similar claim to what Tim made at the custody trial. Tim also told them that he received alarming calls from a restricted number along with text messages threatening his life, insinuating the threats came from Donovan or someone associated with Nicki. FamilyWise did not notify Nicki about those comments. She learned of them while reading their notes after the fact.

The FamilyWise supervisor noted during visits when Callahan would say he couldn't wait "to come home" with Tim. The notes of conversations between Cal and Tim made it clear that Tim had established his house as "home" and had expressed to his son his hope that one day, Nicki and Cal would return to him, reuniting their "family."

"Mommy still can't come home," Callahan said to his dad, according to the supervisor's notes. "Someday, she will change her mind. That will happen someday, I bet."

On the first visit following Cal's fifth birthday, Tim used the opportunity to paint Nicki negatively and put her in a difficult position. Tim used the official communication channels to ask Nicki if he could bring Cal a birthday present, and she agreed. Yet, when Callahan asked Tim about the gift, Tim told the boy his mom would have to bring him to Tim's house to get it. That led to Cal continuously asking his mom if they could go over to Tim's house to get the birthday present.

Tim appeared to be repeating his interrogation tactics during his visits, asking, "Is there anything else you want to tell me, buddy?" multiple times without the monitor intervening. They were supposed to redirect him from his past patterns.

Nicki felt FamilyWise workers had been negative toward her since the start. That feeling was proven in an email Glorina sent to Tim's attorney as they neared six months of supervised visits.

"In all my professional years of working with families, I am shocked that a parent is allowed to bring forth such claims which feel as though they are making attempts at parental alienation," Glorina wrote, referring to Nicki—not Tim. "Frankly, there have been zero interactions over the past six months from Mr. Amacher that have given us pause."

Less than one month remained before the judge would consider allowing Cal to stay at Tim's home unsupervised once again. Glorina forwarded to Tim's attorney other emails written by Nicki's lawyer, Stacy Lofgren, that asked the facility to address Nicki's concerns stemming from the visits. Glorina was frustrated with Nicki and Stacy. She wrote to Tim's lawyer that she doubted FamilyWise could continue to serve them.

"Honestly, this is a case in which—as I explained—may need to be discharged due to the consistent and seemingly unrealistic expectations and consistent complaints by the other party," Glorina wrote.

Nicki filed motions with the court asking Referee Clysdale to extend the supervised visitation period. However, it appeared that within the confines of court-ordered supervised visitation, Tim still somehow managed to build a case for restoring his access to Callahan.

CHAPTER TWENTY-TWO

Tim petitioned the court in December 2021 to resume overnight visits with Callahan unsupervised at his home. For exhibits, he filed the email from Glorina Fruetel—the supervised parenting program manager at FamilyWise—as well as supervisor notes from the visits. Tim highlighted each example where Cal repeated past claims that originated from his coaching along with each example where Cal stated he wanted to "go home" with Tim.

Tim stated he had gone six months without making accusations or recording his son, which Nicki and her attorney, Stacy Lofgren, thought was debatable. In addition, Tim accused Nicki and Stacy of attempting to micromanage FamilyWise's rules through constant contact.

Stacy and Nicki pointed out that Tim refused to pay for the court-ordered parenting coach, attempting to use his existing therapist for that purpose until the judge directed him to hire a separate professional. They focused much of their response on showing Referee Elizabeth Clysdale the positive effect the diminished chaos after the switch to supervised visitation was having on Callahan. The boy's therapist noted that Cal felt safer due to the way the visits with his father were structured compared to how their time was spent before. It should come as no surprise that Cal enjoyed visits, which consisted completely of one-on-one playtime with his dad.

Referee Clysdale, however, decided that Tim had reached her required benchmarks. After a hearing in late January, she ruled that "upon review of the FamilyWise notes, there is no reason not to transition Father's parenting time to unsupervised parenting time." She decided to transition slowly before allowing overnight visits. Cal's first unsupervised visit would take place the following Saturday from 11:00 a.m. to 5:00 p.m. After two months of visits like those each week, if everything went well, Tim could work his way up to overnight stays.

Nicki drove Callahan to the police station in Saint Paul that they had used as a parental exchange spot during the COVID-19 pandemic when FamilyWise was closed. She nearly asked her mom to handle the exchange for her, but Nicki doubted Tim would be there. She figured he would send Colleen on his behalf, but sure enough, Tim was already there waiting when Nicki arrived early for the drop-off.

Before Nicki could unbuckle Cal from his car seat and carry him to Tim's vehicle, Tim got out and met her between their vehicles.

"Do you want to go get breakfast with us? We should sit down and talk. I really think you and I need to be on the same page as we co-parent Cal," Tim said.

Nicki was dumbfounded. After everything they had just gone through with the custody trial, the false reports, and the orders for protection, here Tim was—smiling—and inviting her out to eat as if nothing between them had occurred.

"Just get in my car, so we can talk," Tim continued as they stood in the parking lot on the January morning. "Obviously, a lot has happened between us. But we really need to come together for Callahan. I have a lot of questions, and I'm sure you have a lot of questions for me. I think you and I really need to sit down and talk this through."

What is he trying to do? Nicki wondered.

The first thought that crossed Nicki's mind was that Tim was secretly recording her and trying to get her to say something he could somehow use against her in the future.

"I don't really feel comfortable with that," Nicki answered. "I agree it would be great for us to have a conversation, but I'm not anywhere near ready for that after everything that's happened."

As Tim started buckling Callahan into the car seat in his vehicle, Tim began telling Cal about their plans for the day, "Daddy wanted Mommy to come, but Mommy didn't want to."

"Look, it's not that I'm not open to talking to you, but this is not a good time for it, and I am nowhere near ready for that conversation at this moment," Nicki repeated.

"Well, whenever you're ready, we could get a meal or a coffee," Tim said. "Whatever we need to do to make this happen, we have to talk about stuff."

There was not even the slightest part of Nicki that believed Tim had changed. When she met Anya for brunch right after the exchange, it dawned on her what must have been going through Tim's head.

He doesn't know Donovan is back.

Tim didn't learn Donovan had moved back to Colorado until his last false sex abuse claim in March 2021. With more than a year passing between Donovan's move and this parental exchange, Tim thought there was a good chance Donovan and Nicki had broken up. That's the conclusion Nicki and Anya reached as they talked during their brunch about the strange interaction.

What Tim didn't know, however, is that two months earlier, in November 2021, Donovan had moved back to Minnesota. He had been living with Nicki since then. As the hours passed that afternoon during Tim's unsupervised visit with Callahan, Nicki felt uneasy. Besides feeling—based on their interaction—that Tim was plotting another reconciliation attempt, Callahan hadn't been alone with Tim for many months. Nicki was worried about how the visit itself was going.

When she arrived back at the police station to pick up Cal at 5:00 p.m., everything about Tim's demeanor was different. He cruised in and hurriedly walked Callahan over to Nicki's car. As she began saying, "Hey, Cal, how was it?" Tim interrupted her. "Have a good day, Lenway."

He then turned and walked away. Countless times during their relationship, when they would fight and Tim was angry with her, he would call Nicki by her last name. Coming from him, it was not a term of endearment.

Just before 10 p.m. that night, Nicki and Donovan were watching TV when her doorbell rang. Two Burnsville Police Officers stood there—an experienced sergeant and a young patrol officer—and they explained that Tim had made another report of sexual abuse against Donovan.

Tim must have found out Donovan moved back, Nicki immediately thought.

As the two officers stood at the door with Tim's fresh accusation, terror raced through Donovan. What if—just like the White Bear Lake officer who had taken Tim's word about the

SUV versus Foot incident and charged Nicki with no context—these Burnsville cops hadn't done their homework? With Donovan living under the same roof as Cal, the possibility of being arrested on the spot because of a false claim was much higher, and the gravity of the accusation could end his career.

Thankfully, before arriving at Nicki's house, the experienced sergeant had researched the past cases his department had handled regarding Tim. He explained that, of course, they would need to fully investigate. But he assured Donovan and Nicki that he was well aware of Tim's history. The officers came inside and checked on Cal in his bedroom.

"I'm good," the boy told the police officers.

The police felt confident Callahan was safe. They told Nicki and Donovan that Tim said something to his parenting coach alleging sexual abuse by Donovan. As a mandatory reporter, the parenting coach then called 911.

Tim made his allegation via email after he dropped off Cal at the end of the visit. Tim framed his reasons for writing to her as though he were using her as a sounding board for frustrations, which she previously advised him to do. Tim wrote that during their visit, Callahan told him graphic stories of molestation.

"Donovan will sneak into my room upstairs by Mama's room," Tim wrote that Cal told him. "This completely threw me off, as Donovan's name hasn't come up in a long time, plus I was told he lives outside the state. Cal continued with, 'Mama always tells me it's in my head and I'm making it up, but Mama has done it too and watched Donovan do it.'"

"Oh wow, Tim. This is so specific and horrendous," the parenting coach responded. "Know that you are his buffer from the trauma and that I will be making a report."

"Please don't report! The referee will say I did a false report, and I will have him ripped from me again," Tim emailed back. "What kind of father am I if I can't help my own son?"

"I'm mandated to report," the parenting coach emailed back. "You are a fabulous father. This is so painful, but we cannot ignore it."

The next morning, Nicki confirmed with Cal that his dad had asked him about Donovan, and that Cal told Tim that Donovan was living with them. Beyond that, Cal described how Tim "reminded" him how Donovan and Nicki had both abused Cal before.

"Daddy showed me pictures and videos," Cal said. "So, Daddy can't be lying."

The boy explained that when his dad brought up the topic of abuse, Cal couldn't remember his mom and Donovan hurting him. So Tim showed him pictures and videos—including Tim's interviews with Cal, where the boy parroted what his dad was saying—to "prove it" to him. Nicki could tell Callahan wanted to tell her about it but didn't want to hurt her feelings. He also worried about what Tim would think.

"Please don't tell Daddy because I think he'd be mad that I'm telling," Callahan said. "Daddy maked me say these things because Daddy doesn't think I'm telling the truth. Daddy is older, so he's smarter and knows more."

Nicki was shocked and at a loss for what to say to her son. She reiterated that he was safe and that neither she nor Donovan had ever hurt him. They never would hurt him.

Two days later, Cal stayed overnight with his grandma and grandpa. The boy told Rae he had something he wanted to tell her.

"But I'm afraid you will hate me if I do," Cal said.

"I could never hate you no matter what, and you can tell me anything," Rae said.

"I said something that wasn't true. I told someone that Mommy and Donovan hurt me," Cal said.

"Did Mommy or Donovan ever hurt you?" Rae asked.

"No," Cal said.

"Who did you tell this to?" Rae asked.

"Daddy," Cal said.

"Why would you say that?" Rae asked.

"Because Daddy wanted me to say it, and I want to make Daddy happy," Cal said.

"I understand because I like to make people happy, too. But remember that it's always important to tell the truth," Rae said.

"I know. I'm sorry," Cal said.

Rae assured her grandson that it was OK and that everyone made mistakes. Cal told her that he loved her and hugged his grandma tighter than he ever had before. Rae's heart hurt from the conversation—Cal telling her in his own words how he was struggling emotionally.

Burnsville Police scheduled one last forensic interview with Callahan to be conducted by Detective Andrea Newton, who had reviewed all of the history in the case, along with social worker Johannah Bradle. When they finished, they informed Nicki that Callahan was very straightforward with them and told them that neither Nicki nor Donovan had ever hurt him. Cal thought his dad wanted him to say those things in order to get more time with him. Cal also told the officer and social worker that he thought Tim wanted him to say those things so Donovan would move out, adding, "Maybe I should tell Daddy that Donovan is nice next time I see him."

As soon as Detective Newton's interview was complete, Nicki filed an emergency motion to suspend Tim's parenting time for putting Callahan in emotional, psychological, and/or physical danger. Referee Clysdale signed the order the very next day and scheduled a court hearing two weeks later.

In response, Tim blamed his parenting coach, Tina Feigal, calling her "an overzealous advocate." She actually believed the things Tim told her throughout their sessions, and that backfired for him. Tina reported more than what was in Tim's email—telling police about the "background information" Tim had told her in their sessions together, including already debunked lies about past abuse and ritualistic molestation. Tim had told Tina that Referee Clysdale was racist and admitted to him off the record that she purposely rules against him because Tim is Black and Nicki is white. Angry that his lies were now before Referee Clysdale, Tim said he planned to look for a different parenting coach.

At the court hearing on February 9, 2022, Referee Clysdale was struck by Tim's lack of change. Even after completing the tasks and following the rules she put forth in her custody order after the trial, Tim gained no self-awareness and insight into how he was harming his son. It was plain to the judge that Tim was hurting his son emotionally. She rejected his unsupervised parenting time, forcing a return to FamilyWise. This time, rather than splitting the cost of the supervised visits, Tim would have to pay for it himself.

When Tim's unsupervised access to Callahan was removed, Nicki once again felt safer. Weeks went by as the calendar inched closer to the next check-in at court. When Nicki returned to FamilyWise on April 20, 2022, at the end of Tim's fifth supervised visit under the new order, she didn't know how completely the change had pushed him over the edge. She didn't know that by the end of that night, she'd be fighting for her life—and her chance to ever see Callahan again.

CHAPTER

TWENTY-THREE

"Who's shot? Where's the victim?" a Minneapolis Police Officer called out, running toward FamilyWise after being dispatched to a shots-fired call at 7:33 p.m. on April 20, 2022. The busy scene seemed out of place, as traffic flowed along University Avenue as if nothing was wrong, yet bystanders screamed for help from where the shooting very publicly happened on the sidewalk in daylight. A woman crying hysterically pointed Officer Joseph Sullivan to the passenger window of Emilie Clancy's gray SUV, still parked just feet away from where Nicki was shot.

"Oh my God, oh my God, oh my God!" cried the bystander, who was there herself to pick up a child from FamilyWise. "Her son is still in the building for a supervised visit."

Nicki lay reclined in the passenger seat in the heroic stranger's arms. Emilie and Nicki's eyes were locked, concentrating on breathing together. Emilie held pressure on Nicki's neck wound with one hand and wrapped her other arm around Nicki's head to comfort her. Emilie tried to stay calm as she relayed information to the officer,

"She got shot in the neck and in the arm," Emilie calmly told Officer Sullivan.

"We've got EMS on the way," Officer Sullivan told them.

Emilie continued comforting Nicki, "You're doing great."

Officer Sullivan noticed two spots on Nicki's arm where feather stuffing protruded from her coat—on the lower sleeve where a bullet traveled straight through Nicki's forearm and blood trickled down to her hand, and on the upper sleeve where either a third bullet or shrapnel shot through the coat and narrowly missed Nicki's arm. The officer started cutting Nicki's coat sleeve near the forearm wound when an ambulance pulled up behind them.

"Right here, this is the victim right here," he shouted to emergency medical service personnel. "First name Nicki, gunshot wound to the neck."

None of the first responders recognized the victim, whom they might have worked alongside at some point at other crime scenes. Nicki managed to pull out her driver's license and give it to Officer Sullivan as the paramedic helped her to her feet.

Remarkably, while suffering from two gunshot wounds, Nicki was still able to walk with assistance twenty-five steps from Emilie's vehicle to the ambulance parked behind them and lie down on a stretcher. Blood did not appear to be actively flowing out of the hole in her neck, but paramedics had no idea how close the bullet had passed by a major artery. One micron in either direction, and Nicki would have bled out on the sidewalk before the ambulance arrived.

"Does she know who shot her?" Officer Peter Bacon asked as soon as he arrived.

Nicki shook her head in response as the paramedics loaded her into the ambulance.

"She hasn't spoken at all," Officer Sullivan said.

Officer Bacon's partner jumped into the ambulance to ride to the hospital with Nicki. While on the way, Nicki began feeling excruciating pain in her ribs from the bullet shot through her neck that remained inside her.

Officers Bacon and Sullivan walked back to the parking lot of FamilyWise, where Emilie was standing with the other bystander, who introduced herself to the police as Megan Curran. Megan had gotten to know Nicki by crossing paths in the parking lot every other week as they picked up their kids.

"My friend Nicki and I both have kids here at this supervised visit center. So whoever did this knows she was coming to pick up her kid at 7:30," Megan said. "We get out of our car and go pick them up at 7:30. I was just going, and she was ahead of me. I could see from the car, the hoodie, the black hoodie, and someone shooting."

"Just a guy with a dark hoodie?" Officer Sullivan asked.

"I couldn't tell if it was a guy or a girl, but a dark hoodie," Megan said.

As Megan began to show Officer Sullivan how the shooting took place, he noticed three spent cartridge casings on the ground, along with three unspent shells the shooter apparently dropped.

After talking with Emilie, Officer Bacon directed a FamilyWise employee to check the surveillance video. Both officers noticed several cameras installed on the sides of the building. Those cameras, along with others in the neighborhood, would provide the evidence they needed to begin identifying the shooter.

CHAPTER TWENTY-FOUR

After Nicki was taken to the hospital, and the crime scene outside the supervised parenting center was secure, Minneapolis Police Officers asked FamilyWise staff to bring Tim into the lobby with them. He was wearing a black baseball cap, COVID mask, and jacket, along with a dark t-shirt and jeans.

"Right now, I'm going to ask if I can search you for weapons really quick," Sergeant Brandon Noble asked in a friendly, almost apologetic tone.

"For weapons?" Tim asked incredulously, raising his arms to the side. "Why would I have weapons in here?"

After patting Tim down, Sergeant Noble cut straight to the point.

"So, your ex-partner was involved in a shooting right outside here," he said.

"A shooting?" Tim asked.

Tim initially acted surprised by the news, but his reactions that followed looked suspicious to the police. Sergeant Noble explained that his fellow officers in the lobby wanted to talk with Tim at the downtown department headquarters. Tim didn't ask if Nicki was OK. He didn't ask any questions about how the shooting took place. He immediately began running down his list of grievances against Minneapolis Police.

"I've been threatened by Minneapolis Police. I've been told, 'Stay out of Minneapolis, or I'm going to catch one.' I have a recording of an interview with Sergeant Amy Walker, and she said the interview never happened. I went to internal affairs twice. So for, you know, my ex and her coworkers to say I'm going to be OK going with police downtown for an interview when I haven't even done anything—I mean—I don't know what this has to do with me," Tim said.

The other officers kept their poker faces despite how odd they thought it sounded for Tim to say, "I don't know what this has to do with me," after the mother of his child was shot right outside the door where this conversation was taking place. They tried to convince Tim that their body cameras would remain on. They promised him nothing would happen to him.

"Like I said, I've been pulled over and threatened by your fellow officers. I've been threatened by an officer before I went into court to testify about Nicki striking me down with her car. I just don't want anything to do with it," Tim said.

"Look, there was a shooting that happened here," one officer began to say.

"Which has nothing to do with me," Tim interrupted.

"That's why we want to get you interviewed, get you out of here, get out on your way," the officer finished.

"I've been here the whole time. I don't know what happened out there," Tim answered, motioning out the window. "You said there was a shooting? I didn't even hear gunshots in here."

Officers are trained to pick up on behavioral clues. What difference would it make whether Tim heard or didn't hear gunshots? It seemed to them like a classic distancing tactic guilty parties subconsciously use.

When Tim offered to speak to officers in Saint Paul instead, the officer chuckled at the absurdity of the suggestion and said, "But it happened right out here."

After a few seconds of silence, while Tim was handing his ID to the officer, he finally asked, "Is everyone OK?"

"We don't know for sure," the officer responded.

"Shit, that sucks," Tim said.

After a few more moments of silence, Tim strangely asked the officers if they wanted to hear his recording of Sergeant Amy Walker from one of his visits to the internal affairs office, which he had already mentioned twice within the five-minute conversation. The officers sensed Tim was trying to pivot the conversation to anything other than the shooting that had just taken place outside. They weren't trying to interview him. That would be the job of the detectives back at police headquarters.

"I'm going to ask you politely if you could please willingly go with me. Would you be willing to go down there? Otherwise, we're going to take you in cuffs," Sergeant Noble said.

"That's so unfair. This is completely unjust," Tim complained before finally going along with the officers.

While riding in the back of the police squad car to the department headquarters, Tim repeated his cycle of accusations of being threatened by Minneapolis Police and not being taken seriously by an internal affairs investigator then feigning surprise that police would want to talk to him concerning the shooting at FamilyWise. He then started on his false claims concerning Callahan.

"So, my son's getting molested. How come this type of seriousness wasn't taken toward him?" Tim oddly stated to the two officers in front, apparently out of the blue during the car ride. "I just don't get why I'm being pulled into all this. I'm minding my own business, trying to watch my son, and I get dragged into something that has nothing to do with me. It's really, really, really frustrating."

The two officers driving the squad car tried to maintain a friendly rapport, constantly reminding Tim they were the last two police to arrive at the crime scene, and their job was just to drive him downtown. They didn't engage Tim with any substantive questions, but Tim continued to vent to them.

"Once again, it's like all stops are being pulled out. I'm being pulled in probably because she asked you guys, 'Hey, drag him down there, give them shit.' It's pretty sad. Nicole Lenway or Donovan Ford or whoever's outside FamilyWise. I don't even know who's outside because I don't know who picks Callahan up. Could even be Nicki's mom," Tim said.

Over the course of the rest of his interactions with police that night, Tim would repeat that he didn't know who picked up Cal from FamilyWise. Police thought it was another part of his smokescreen. Tim also injected claims of racism, noting all the "white faces" surrounding him, threatening arrest, and asking him about something he did not do.

As Tim was led into an interview room at the Minneapolis Police headquarters, acting irritated, he once again repeated his loop of grievances, going deeper into the details of his false allegations of sexual abuse of Cal by Nicki and Donovan.

"I mean, my son has made reports, like my son literally called his mom out at her house in front of the CPS worker saying, 'You play with my penis. You want me to say Daddy hurts me. Daddy never hurts me. Hey, do you wanna see where mommy keeps the stick that she beats me with? Come in here. Let me show you.' Did anybody do anything about that?"

Officers grew more impatient with Tim but tried not to show it.

Minneapolis Police Sergeant Mark Suchta walked into the interview room. He's known for being one of the best at MPD at keeping a stone face and even keel demeanor. When Tim restarted his complaint loop, Sergeant Suchta cut him off.

"You know that Nicki was shot, right?"

"No," Tim said. "I didn't even know she was down there because I don't know if she goes down there, the mom goes down there, one of her boyfriends goes down. I don't know anything. No, I do not know that she's…"

"Just so you know, Nicki was shot. She was shot in the neck. She's in stable condition right now, but it's very serious," the detective said, noticing Tim's not-so-subtle dig at the victim with his "one-of-her-boyfriends" remark.

Even though Sergeant Noble told Tim in the FamilyWise lobby that his ex-partner was involved in a shooting, Tim seemed intent on cementing the narrative that no one told him Nicki was shot and that he didn't even know Nicki was present at FamilyWise. His story cracked slightly when Sergeant Suchta persisted.

"When did you hear about all this? Did anyone tell you that Nicki was shot?" Sergeant Suchta asked.

"No, nothing," Tim said.

"So, coming down here, you had no idea Nicki had been shot?" Sergeant Suchta asked again in a surprised tone.

"No," Tim replied before adding that after he learned about gunshots, the FamilyWise supervisor told him Nicki had ducked down in her car when shots rang out and that she was fine. Sergeant Suchta moved on to his next question.

"Do you have any idea at all who would have shot Nicki?"

"Absolutely," Tim responded.

"Who?" Sergeant Suchta asked.

The detective knew that Tim's answer to that question would likely be a preview of his criminal defense if eventually arrested as the mastermind of Nicki's shooting.

CHAPTER TWENTY-FIVE

When Sergeant Mark Suchta asked Tim who he thought might have shot Nicki, it was a question Tim had clearly been anticipating. He began explaining the internal affairs interview with Minneapolis Police Sergeant Amy Walker that he claimed to have recorded, which he clearly hoped someone would ask him more about. Tim asserted that he had informed Sergeant Walker that Nicki confessed to him that she tampered with evidence in one of the high-profile crimes she worked on as a forensic scientist for MPD.

The 2015 police shooting of Jamar Clark was a controversial case in Minneapolis as protesters camped out in front of the precinct on the north side for two weeks, demanding the officers involved be charged. The two officers were eventually cleared of any criminal wrongdoing, as DNA evidence proved Clark grabbed one of the officers' guns during the preceding struggle.

Tim wanted Sergeant Suchta to bite on his claim that Nicki tampered with evidence in that case. While she did collect evidence at the crime scene that night, another agency handled the processing of it, including swabbing for DNA. None of it mattered to Sergeant Suchta as he sat there expressionless, waiting for Tim to stop talking, not believing a word that came out of his mouth as he continued.

"I remember that was a big deal. She was afraid because she thought people were driving by her house. She changed her last name to her middle name. She shut down her social media. She had drive-bys of Minneapolis Police coming to her house all the time. She had me bring over my shotgun to her house. She was in fear," Tim claimed.

When the detective asked Tim who else he thought might have shot Nicki, Tim began expressing some concern about her condition but continued making patronizing comments about Nicki. Tim told Sergeant Suchta that Nicki had multiple affairs with police officers. He mentioned the graffiti on her garage door. He suggested that the police talk to social worker Theresa Roberts and the supervisors at FamilyWise, claiming they are the only ones who have been neutral observers of all the issues that happened between Tim and Nicki.

It wasn't lost on Sergeant Suchta that, at that point, he hadn't accused Tim of doing anything. All the defensive responses from Tim and unsolicited insults about Nicki were extremely suspicious, considering she was in the hospital fighting for her life. Suchta asked Tim if he would give police permission to search his Jeep, which was still parked at FamilyWise. Tim responded that he would only allow the search if they let him watch, adding that police wouldn't find anything unless they planted evidence.

"Unless they're throwing stuff in there, man!" Tim laughed, posing his statement—like many he made that night—as a joke.

Sergeant Suchta did not laugh.

Tim reluctantly allowed the detective to look through his cell phone, including deleted messages, to see who he had called and texted that night. Finding nothing, Sergeant Suchta did not seize the phone. Toward the end of their short interview, Tim offered Sergeant Suchta more unsolicited, condescending advice on how to solve the case.

"I don't know what you guys do here, if you guys have little buddy-buddy talks," Tim said. "I'd talk to Nicki like a buddy and say, 'Dude, if you're doing something, let me know so we can protect you.'"

Sergeant Suchta cut Tim off before he could continue, asking him for the correct spelling of his name and telling the patrol officers to bring Tim back to FamilyWise.

Back at the parking lot where his Jeep remained, Tim once again started reciting many of the same lines he'd used all night. When officers asked Tim to reaffirm his permission for them to search his car without a warrant, he started acting irritated and impatient.

While officers opened doors and started looking inside, Tim inserted himself, reaching around them and sliding seats around—an exaggerated demonstration that he wasn't hiding anything. Tim's Jeep had been parked under a surveillance camera at FamilyWise since he arrived before 6:00 p.m. If he indeed was involved in a premeditated attempt to kill Nicki, it was extremely unlikely he would have any evidence in that vehicle.

After police finished the search, another detective, Sergeant Marcus Benner, walked up and asked a question that would prove critical to the investigation. It seemed to be the one question all night that Tim wasn't expecting.

"Are there any other vehicles on file, or this is it?" Sgt. Benner asked.

"Yeah, this is mine," Tim stammered.

"This is your only car?" Sgt. Benner immediately followed up.

"Yep," Tim answered without hesitation. Then, after looking away and pausing a couple of seconds, Tim asked, "Wait, what do you mean?"

"This is your only car?" Sergeant Benner asked again.

"No, no," Tim said. "I have a Dodge Challenger, too. It's under a tarp, though."

Sergeant Benner filed away Tim's hesitant answer to the basic question. The investigator had been taught long ago that it's always a good idea to find out how many and what types of vehicles a potential suspect owns or has access to. Benner already knew of a suspicious vehicle Tim had conveniently left out.

As the clock struck 10:00 p.m., just two and a half hours after Nicki was shot, police told Tim he was free to go home. There was not enough probable cause to arrest him. They observed and noted his demeanor and answers while being treated as a witness rather than a suspect, which would be very important in assessing his possible role in the crime. When Tim strutted back toward his Jeep, one of the officers who had been friendliest to him all night made one last statement, to which Tim could not resist hissing back an angry response.

"Tim, Tim, Tim. Sorry we met under this circumstance, all right?"

"I just wish the same enthusiasm that you guys are using for one of your own, that you guys would use for a little, Black, five-year-old that's been getting molested," Tim said before he drove away from the scene of the crime.

CHAPTER TWENTY-SIX

Rae and Joe Lenway were waiting for Nicki to drop off Callahan for the night, so she could leave for work. She typically would arrive at their house at 8:00 p.m. so that she could leave by 8:15 or 8:20 for her shift at MPD. As a mother, Rae's anxiety concerning any sort of late arrival had been heightened ever since Chantal's death, so by the time the clock showed 8:05, she was already nervous.

Maybe they stopped for gas or a treat or something, Rae tried to reassure herself.

At 8:15, Rae's phone rang. It was Donovan.

"What are you doing?" Donovan asked.

"Just waiting for Nicki," Rae responded.

"You need to leave immediately and go to Hennepin County Medical Center. Nicole's been shot," Donovan calmly informed her.

Pin-pricks of panic began tingling throughout Rae's body.

"What?" she asked.

"She's been shot. She's at HCMC. You need to go there now," Donovan repeated.

As she and Joe got into the car, Rae called Donovan back to ask about Callahan. After Tim's final false report one month earlier, Donovan moved out of Nicki's house and into his own place. There, Donovan had been sleeping after a long work shift of his own when he received a phone call from a coworker and friend to inform him of the shooting. Not having all the information, he didn't realize Nicki had not yet picked up Callahan when she was shot outside FamilyWise.

"I thought he was with you!" Donovan said, promising Rae he'd make sure his fellow Minneapolis Police Officers knew not to let Tim Amacher leave with the boy.

Rae and Joe arrived at the hospital, where a large group of uniformed and plain-clothed officers were standing vigil. After about an hour of waiting, the couple was led into the room where a trauma doctor was still with Nicki.

Nicki lay in the bed unconscious and wearing a green gown. Her neck was stabilized in a cervical collar. She was intubated with a tracheal tube attached to her neck to breathe for her. Machines monitored her vitals, and an IV dripped painkillers and nutrients into her body. Another machine was keeping Nicki's lung inflated after it collapsed from the primary bullet that entered through her neck. Nicki's right arm was bandaged from the other gunshot and stabilized with straps to prevent her from accidentally harming herself if she awoke.

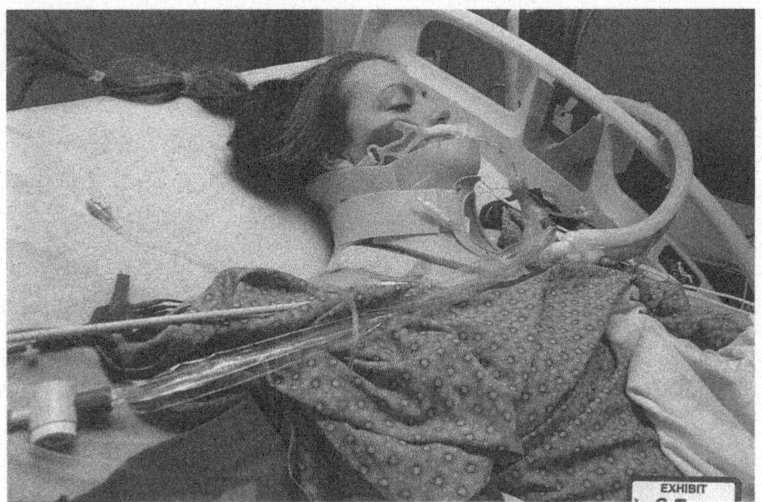

Nicki hospitalized after being shot. Courtroom Exhibit.

Doctors discovered that the bullet entered the right side of Nicki's neck and cut her larynx or voice box, resulting in swelling and internal bruising that necessitated the breathing tube. Swelling of the voice box can sometimes be serious enough to block the airway and cause death. That bullet was still lodged in Nicki's ribs, and doctors believed it would be safer to leave it there than try to remove it. The other bullet that struck Nicki's forearm near her wrist went straight through, fracturing her radial bone.

Rae walked to the side of the bed by Nicki's left, wrapped herself around that free arm, clutched her hand, and began talking to her.

"We have Cal. It's going to be OK," Rae said to her motionless daughter.

They actually did not yet have the young boy, but a sergeant at the hospital had told the couple an officer was caring for Callahan and arranging to bring him to them. Rae knew that would be Nicki's top concern, so she attempted to comfort her.

"You focus on you. You get better. You save your strength and recover, and don't worry about Cal. He's OK. We've got him," Rae continued.

Joe gently piped in, telling his wife, "She can't hear you."

And the doctor corrected him, saying, "Oh, no, she absolutely can hear you. There is brain activity, so she can hear you."

He was right. As Nicki lay motionless, hooked up to machines and monitors, she felt like she was having a dream she was unable to awaken from—the universal nightmare where you find yourself moving in slow motion and without working vocal cords. She tried with all her might to open her eyes, to let out a sound, and to squeeze her mother's hand.

And that's when Rae felt it—the faintest, teeny-tiny squeeze. A muscle twitch, more or less. But it was enough for Rae to know her daughter was attempting to communicate with them.

Up until that point, Rae thought she was going to lose her last living daughter. She was distraught for the entire ride to HCMC, thinking that soon, both of her children would be dead. But—after feeling Nicki's responsive grip—Rae confidently told Joe, "She's going to be OK. She's fighting. She squeezed my hand!"

As the doctor led Rae and Joe out of the room, explaining the upcoming surgeries she would need, Donovan was finally allowed inside. He was one of the first to arrive at the hospital and was right outside Nicki's room for at least ten painful minutes as doctors worked to save her life.

Donovan approached Nicki gently, walking up to her right side where her arm that was shot was heavily bandaged. His own body felt drained by all the emotions of the evening.

"I love you. Hang in there," he quietly said to Nicki.

Then, like a scene from a scary movie, Nicki's eyes popped open upon hearing Donovan's voice, and she jolted up, sitting in bed and trying to hug him.

"Whoa, whoa, whoa," Donovan reassured her, his heart racing from the jump scare. "I'm here, but you need to lie down."

Donovan was ushered out of the hospital room after his own brief visit, telling Nicki he loved her and assuring her that she would be OK. Nicki's reactions to hearing Donovan and Rae's voices helped put their minds slightly more at ease, knowing she was fighting.

On the way out of the locked intensive care ward where Nicki was checked in as "Jane Doe" for her safety, Rae and Joe learned Callahan was just arriving. Lieutenant Kelly O'Rourke pulled into the emergency room driveway in a squad car, hopped out before opening the passenger door, and told the Lenways, "He doesn't know anything. We didn't tell him anything."

Callahan got out of the police car and told his grandma and grandpa how Lieutenant O'Rourke had let him activate the lights and the sirens. Then he looked around.

"Where's Mom?" he asked. "Mom was supposed to come get me."

"Well, Mom's in the hospital," Rae said, explaining to the boy that he couldn't immediately see his mom because the doctors needed to work on her.

"What happened?" Callahan asked.

Rae remembered that the officers who shared details of the shooting with her said that Nicki fell to the ground after she was shot but then got up and ran. That gave Rae an idea for the basic explanation she could give the inquisitive five-year-old.

"Well, I don't know for sure what happened, buddy, but I know she fell to the ground, and she got hurt. So, the doctors are going to tell us more later," Rae said.

"Can I talk to her?" Callahan asked.

"No, she hurt her throat, so she can't talk right now," Rae said.

Callahan accepted the explanation, telling his grandparents he wanted to talk to her as soon as her throat was better. After getting into the car, Callahan began to cry in the backseat.

"I just really miss my mom. I want to see my mom," he said.

The drive back home was teary-eyed for all of them as Rae and Joe did their best to comfort their grandson while they held onto hope that Nicki would indeed be OK.

CHAPTER
TWENTY-SEVEN

Nicki woke up in her hospital bed early the next morning, thinking to herself, *Did this really happen?* She immediately wondered if she was having another one of her nightmares where Tim escapes with Callahan.

The events of the previous twelve hours started coming back to her in flashes. Sitting up in the stretcher and recognizing the HCMC ambulance bay. The blinding lights of the emergency department. Her parents' calming voices inside the hospital room. Then—the thin female shooter.

Nicki's thoughts were interrupted by the shocking feeling of restriction and gag reflex as she choked on her breathing tubes. As hospital staff delivered the news to Minneapolis Police that Nicki had awakened, two detectives went straight to her hospital room and gave her a Sharpie pen and paper.

"I knew he would do something like this," the right-handed shooting victim scribbled with her uninjured left hand.

Through a series of notes and facial expressions, the mute crime scene investigator attempted to convey a timeline of her past relationship with Tim from when they first met in 2012. Nicki wrote that Tim claimed they continued dating long after their actual breakup, and she wrote about the police and CPS reports he filed against her.

The two Minneapolis Police Detectives—Sergeant Michael Heyer and Sergeant James Jensen—had already viewed the surveillance video from FamilyWise. The video showed Nicki exiting her car and briskly walking toward the building while looking at her phone. A slim person dressed in all black can be seen sprinting down the sidewalk from nearly a block away, pulling out a handgun behind Nicki and firing just off-camera. Another surveillance angle from down the street captured how the shooter continued advancing on Nicki while she crawled on the ground desperately trying to get away.

Three minutes before the shooting, just after Nicki drove into the parking lot, the FamilyWise surveillance video showed that the same person dressed in black with a white medical mask apparently took a "dry run." The suspect could be seen casually walking down the sidewalk toward the front door of FamilyWise with their hands in their pockets before turning around and walking back up the block. It appeared the shooter was checking whether Nicki was sitting in her car. Sergeant Heyer and Sergeant Jensen were sure the shooting wasn't random or an attempted robbery. Nicki appeared to be targeted.

Nicki described the shooter, conveying that she still believed it was a woman, writing, "Long black hair. Beanie. Mask. Ran down to me from behind. Parking lot area. I turned, she said nothing."

"Does Tim own a gun?" one of the detectives asked Nicki.

"He owns like an arsenal of weapons," Nicki wrote. She remembered how he stashed them in various places around his Saint Paul house, including the room where their son slept. She remembered him wearing cross-body holsters visible over his tank tops and an ankle holster underneath his jeans as he concealed-carried even during innocuous Sunday morning brunch outings to safe Minneapolis restaurants. Yes, Tim most certainly owned guns. Nicki specified to the detectives that she could think of at least ten different firearms.

I know Tim's behind this, Nicki thought as the two detectives questioned her. *I don't know how, but he's involved.*

Although that seemed obvious, Nicki feared that as the hours ticked away, the investigators hadn't yet put two and two together. Nicki started filling them in on supervised visitation rules. FamilyWise staff was supposed to hold Tim there for an additional fifteen minutes after she left with Callahan, but she knew they weren't following through with that. At the last visit prior to the shooting, Tim pulled up next to Nicki at the very first stoplight after she left the FamilyWise parking lot. Yet, police had confirmed he indeed was inside when the shots were fired.

Sergeant Heyer and Sergeant Jensen then started asking Nicki about Tim's roommate and apparent current girlfriend, Colleen Larson.

"2016 she moved in," Nicki wrote, "supposedly to be Cal's nanny."

As their questions concerning Colleen continued, it was as if a fog began to lift from Nicki's mind.

It's so obvious. How did I not see it before?

Colleen Larson, the meek girl who used to follow Tim around the Taekwondo studio like a puppy—Colleen Larson, with long, dark hair and a slender build, had tried to kill Nicki.

CHAPTER TWENTY-EIGHT

Even though Nicki was a civilian member of the Minneapolis Police Department in its crime lab, as she lay intubated in the hospital as a shooting victim, she wasn't privy to the details of the investigation. Sergeant James Jensen and Sergeant Michael Heyer didn't tell Nicki that after the shooting, FamilyWise staff had given Colleen Larson's name to detectives. The workers knew Colleen from all the times she handled parenting exchanges on Tim's behalf. They told police that, in their opinion, Colleen could easily be influenced by Tim. That analysis rang with irony after all the times the FamilyWise monitors defended Tim.

Colleen was a twenty-four-year-old woman who joined World Taekwondo Academy in White Bear Lake in 2010 when she was thirteen. Tim Amacher, her instructor and mentor, was thirty years old at that time.

The martial art of Taekwondo caught Colleen's interest as she watched her brother Wayne in the classes, and the other students encouraged her to learn Taekwondo to develop much more than just self-defense abilities. They told her it would also help improve other aspects of her life.

Over the next few years, Colleen learned sparring and progressed from a white belt beginner to eventually earning her black belt. To people who knew Colleen, however, she didn't seem capable of harming others. She stood five feet three inches tall and weighed 115 pounds, and to describe Colleen in a single word, many would use "meek."

Colleen Larson at a Taekwondo competition.

Others in the studio noticed the strange progression of the impressionable girl's interactions with her master. John Swoboda, a personal trainer in the gym portion of the building, noticed that Tim had started giving Colleen responsibilities such as helping him teach Taekwondo classes. Those duties progressed into Colleen helping maintain the studio, cleaning, and emptying trash bins. Once Callahan was born, Colleen became Tim's top choice for childcare. He told others he was paying Colleen with free personal training sessions, yet John never saw Tim training her in the gym. John joked to others that Colleen had become his slave. Yet he hoped that characterization wasn't literally true.

By the time she turned eighteen, around the same time Nicki gave birth to Callahan, Colleen had moved in with the man she grew up calling "Master Amacher." Nicki and Rae had brief interactions with Colleen at the many parenting exchanges. During the custody trial four years later, Tim claimed he was not romantically involved with Colleen. That status changed in the fall of 2021 when Tim publicly acknowledged Colleen was his girlfriend.

Tim's neighbor, Charlie, found it odd that Colleen continued calling Tim "Master" even after they were officially dating. She was really nothing like any of the other women he'd been with. Tim told Charlie that Colleen was the easiest relationship he had ever been in. Yet, the relationship was far from equal. Just like when she was a young teen, Colleen looked at Tim like a little girl gazing at her idol. To echo the personal trainer's observation, Charlie, at times, felt like Colleen was more of a servant to Tim than a partner. Again, hearing her call her boyfriend "Master" was hard to get past.

Colleen earned a four-year college degree and worked at a graphics company but still spent a lot of time at World Taekwondo Academy in White Bear Lake. Colleen told friends her dream was to open a bakery.

Soon after Minneapolis news stations began reporting on the April 20 shooting, one of them contacted police about an alarming email they received from Colleen's account three and a half hours before the crime.

"Hello. With today's news on the justice system's unfairness toward people of color and children's well-being, I would like to share the story of a child of color whose mother is being abusive physically, mentally, and sexually. His father, a person of color, is fighting to protect his son but is being denied all parental rights and made out to be the bad guy. My name is Colleen Larson, and I'm reaching out on behalf of Timothy Amacher, a proud Black father to Callahan Amacher, born June 20, 2016," the email began.

Colleen identified herself as Callahan's nanny and laid out in more than six hundred words what essentially had become Tim's side of the custody battle with Nicki that he had been spinning for nearly four years. She included specific allegations of abuse—including claims that Tim possessed photo and video evidence. She accused the judicial decision-makers of racism. And she included a date—an ominous deadline of sorts, by which time she believed something drastic needed to be done.

"June 7, 2022, is the last court date that will strip Mr. Amacher's rights as a parent and prevent him from seeing his son regularly. Mr. Amacher has done nothing but play by the rules and still gets penalized, whereas Ms. Lenway has withheld his son from him multiple times and disobeyed court orders with no repercussions," Colleen wrote.

She ended the email by stating she knew "no other way to help other than getting the word out and hoping the right person can help get Callahan out." She then directed the recipient to contact Tim at his cell phone number.

To investigators, the email simultaneously provided answers and raised questions. They had no doubt Tim was the one behind the shooting plot. *But why would Colleen send an email like this right before carrying out the shooting?* It was possible the message was one last cry for "help" before participating in what inevitably would be a risky and life-changing scheme. And when no WCCO-TV reporters immediately responded to the email with interest in an investigative news story, perhaps the young woman felt that she had to do what Tim wanted.

Another possibility that crossed investigators' minds was whether Tim actually wrote the email himself. Was he so diabolical and narcissistic that, even with having the iron-clad alibi of being monitored inside FamilyWise when the shooting happened, he would present an apparent motive from Colleen and a scenario that she acted alone? Along those same lines, police also debated whether Colleen was so blindly loyal to Tim that she was willing to not just kill for him but martyr herself for him.

Regardless, the narrative conveyed in the email mirrored the same motivation they knew Tim possessed, and it pointed back to Colleen, whose physical description matched the shooting suspect. The investigation was beginning to link together a number of things, beginning with a vehicle Tim conveniently left out in his last conversation with police.

CHAPTER

TWENTY-NINE

Outside of FamilyWise on the night of the shooting, Minneapolis Police homicide detective Sergeant Marcus Benner asked Tim the simple question, "Is this your only car?" and Tim's hesitant answer immediately raised red flags. Sergeant Benner told Sergeant James Jensen and Sergeant Michael Heyer, the lead detectives on the case, that Tim was deceptive in his answer. On his way to the shooting scene, Sergeant Benner pulled records of every vehicle registered in Minnesota under Tim Amacher's name. They included a black 2022 Dodge Ram 1500 pickup truck that he had taken delivery of in January 2022, three months before the shooting. When the lead detectives later reviewed the FamilyWise surveillance video, a black truck with no license plates could be seen driving up the same street four minutes prior to the shooter dressed in black making her "dry run" walking down the sidewalk past Nicki's parked car.

Sergeant Benner contacted Minneapolis Public Schools to request surveillance video from an elementary school building just around the corner from FamilyWise. That video showed the black truck parking just one block from the shooting scene. The same shooter seen on the FamilyWise video then exited from the backseat and walked around the corner toward the parenting center. Five minutes later, that camera view showed the shooter sprint back to the truck while holding a gun, then driving away.

After responding to the shooting on Wednesday, April 20, police officers eventually fanned out and found the 2022 Dodge Ram parked outside Amacher's house. It seemed to match the truck seen on surveillance video except it had a temporary license plate on it. Officers started collecting surveillance video from homes and businesses on the most direct route from Tim's home at 801 Clayland Street in Saint Paul to FamilyWise on University Avenue in Minneapolis, which is about a three-mile drive that can take between seven to fifteen minutes, depending on traffic. At multiple points along that path, cameras captured the black truck driving by. In one video clip, while the truck is stopped at a traffic signal, the footage is clear enough to reveal a female driver, who could be Colleen.

Since the Dodge Ram was brand new, investigators had an idea. The majority of new vehicles come with built-in navigation systems. The technology behind those systems essentially makes the vehicle a cellular device. With a search warrant, police could obtain location data from the truck the same way they do from a suspect's personal cell phone. Through an administrative subpoena, police obtained the IMSI number associated with Tim's truck. Each cellular device has its own IMSI or International Mobile Subscriber Identity, which allows the mobile carrier to identify and authenticate a user to provide services. Cell towers and networks use the IMSI to track the phone. Essentially, the truck itself was one giant cell phone.

Sergeant Jensen had already executed search warrants for Tim and Colleen's cell phone providers, asking for call and text message records plus location data. He then wrote an additional search warrant that would compel AT&T to provide location data based on GPS and the nearest cell phone towers the truck connected to as it moved throughout the day.

In the days that followed, police surveilled Tim and Colleen as they went about their routines, leaving their home in Saint Paul and traveling to the Taekwondo studio in White Bear Lake. Police did not interrogate Tim or Colleen's friends and family as they first wanted to build their case while the prime suspects thought they might have gotten away with it. All the while, Nicki remained in the hospital, hoping her colleagues at the Minneapolis Police Department were getting close to making an arrest.

No other plausible suspect or scenario surfaced. Tim was the only person who wanted Nicki dead, and Colleen seemed to be the only person fitting the description of the shooter plus the profile of someone Tim could convince to help him.

When the cell phone location data, including that from the Dodge truck, came back, it confirmed just what detectives expected. Tim's personal cell phone traveled with him throughout the day, including his drive to FamilyWise, arriving around 5:25 p.m., and his transport by police downtown to be interviewed at 8:31 p.m. In addition, Colleen's cell phone traveled with her throughout the day, including a period of time spent at World Taekwondo Academy from 4:02 p.m. to 6:55 p.m. The email was sent during that time.

That's where the location data of Colleen's phone compared to the location data of the Dodge Ram was critical. After leaving the studio at 6:55, the data showed Colleen's phone and the truck traveling together to the home on Clayland Street. After a few minutes, Colleen's phone apparently stayed there while the truck continued toward FamilyWise, perfectly matching the surveillance images police had already gathered on that route. The detectives' theory was that Colleen most likely left her cell phone at home, knowing it could later be tracked, but didn't realize police could track the Dodge Ram when she drove it to FamilyWise and carried out the shooting. Colleen apparently thought the cell phone at home provided an alibi for her location at the time of the shooting, but the contradicting location data instead provided proof of premeditation.

A full week had passed since the shooting, and police were ready to make their move. A judge signed a new round of search warrants for Tim and Colleen's home, the Taekwondo studio, all surveillance systems at both locations, and the Dodge Ram itself. Evidence already collected from the crime scene included three discharged cartridge casings fired from a .380 caliber gun plus three live .380 rounds on the ground.

At 6:26 a.m., a team of officers carrying a protective shield pounded on the door at 801 Clayland Street. Colleen walked down the entrance steps wearing a gray hoodie and pajama pants, sobbing with her hands up.

"I'm sorry!" Colleen cried as she walked to the officers waiting to arrest her.

CHAPTER THIRTY

Police brought Colleen Larson to the downtown Minneapolis Police headquarters to be interviewed. Despite apologizing as she was being taken into custody, she did not confess to police. Colleen claimed she was home at the time of the shooting along with her cell phone. Police booked her into jail, knowing they had thirty-six hours to file charges against her.

The arrest of Tim Amacher happened much less dramatically, just before Colleen, after he drove from their home in the Dodge Ram. He complained about having to be patted down, handcuffed, and his personal items taken out of his pockets, but then Tim stayed quiet until police brought him downtown to a separate interview room. He was sharply dressed in dark jeans, a leather jacket, and a black t-shirt that said "Straight Outta Taekwondo," using a twist on the familiar "Straight Outta Compton" hip-hop album logo.

Tim Amacher's interrogation. Courtroom Exhibit.

The Taekwondo master sat down after officers removed his handcuffs. The lead detectives on the case, Sergeant James Jensen and Sergeant Michael Heyer, read Tim his rights and told him that some details in the investigation uncovered links to him.

"Well, of course," Tim replied. "I'm gonna be the first guy you guys look at."

"Well, yes, you do have a motive," Sergeant Jensen said.

"I don't have any motive!" Tim laughed, claiming that the custody fight with Nicki was all over with.

"Isn't it true that she has custody?" Sergeant Jensen asked.

"Yeah," Tim acknowledged.

"OK, so, if you wanted custody, wouldn't that be a motive?" Sergeant Jensen asked.

"A motive for what?" Tim asked.

"If she's not around, now you'd have custody of the child, correct?" Sergeant Jensen said.

Tim refused to acknowledge the point the investigator was trying to make, claiming he didn't know that, as Cal's biological father, he'd be next to assume custody if anything happened to Nicki. Seeing early in their interrogation that Tim was evasive even on hypothetical questions, they moved on straight to their new information. They reminded Tim how, on the night of the shooting, he was asked about his vehicles.

"When you talked to Sergeant Benner, he asked you what type of vehicles you owned," Sergeant Jensen said.

"He didn't let me finish," Tim interjected. "He just asked me and then walked away, so I started talking about a Hellcat, and then that was pretty much it. He didn't let me finish. I have two motorcycles. I have a truck that I don't really consider mine; it's on lease."

The two investigators had thoroughly reviewed the body camera video from multiple officers, including Sergeant Marcus Benner, and they knew Benner did not immediately walk away as Tim now described. In fact, the sergeant asked Tim multiple times, and Tim seemingly froze upon being asked. As Tim now finally acknowledged the truck, Sergeant Jensen continued the interview.

"That truck is the one that is of interest to us because we can put it at the scene, and we can put it as the shooter's vehicle," Sergeant Jensen said.

"There's no way!" Tim said.

"Oh yes. There is. There's video of the truck and the suspect," Sergeant Jensen responded.

The detectives proceeded to explain how the IMSI technology works and how they were able to track it. Before Sergeant Jensen revealed the cell phone data showing the truck's path going from Tim's Saint Paul home to the shooting scene, he gave Tim a printed surveillance photo of the Dodge Ram en route.

"That's not my truck. Dead giveaway right here," Tim said, pointing at the photograph. "I have Superman logos."

Tim kept interrupting Sergeant Jensen before he could make his point, explaining that he had applied Superman "S" decals to the sides of his Dodge Ram a couple of weeks earlier. He also asserted that his truck was a GT model, with the GT lettering on the rear quarter panels. Neither the decals nor the GT emblem were visible in the photo Tim was looking at.

"Is there any way for that to be faked?" Tim asked, referring to the IMSI tracker and knowing what was likely to come next. "All I'm saying is, is there a way to fake that? Because there's no way that truck could be there if I'm there with my Jeep."

"Well, that's another question. Who else has access to the truck?" Sergeant Heyer asked.

"Uh, Colleen has access to it," Tim answered.

That was the first time Tim had mentioned Colleen's name to the police. As the detectives probed into how Tim met Colleen, the Taekwondo master did not volunteer the fact that they were currently dating. He characterized her as a fellow instructor at the Taekwondo studio instead of labeling her a girlfriend and former student. Tim reacted very defensively when the detectives asked how young Colleen was when he first met her.

"We kind of heard it was around the time she was eight, nine, ten years old," Sergeant Jensen said.

"Oh, hell no!" Tim shot back.

Still, Tim didn't address the fact he and Colleen were romantically involved until Sergeant Heyer directly asked him how long they'd been in a relationship.

"Oh geez, maybe since like September," Tim answered, claiming they had only been dating for about seven months after living as platonic roommates for five years before that.

"Then let me ask you this: Is there any reason why Colleen would wanna shoot Nicole?" Sergeant Heyer asked.

"Oh, hell no! She wouldn't hurt anybody," Tim emphatically said. "I mean, plus, the timeline wouldn't even really match for her to do anything anyway 'cause she works. She teaches."

"Well, that's where a problem begins as well," Sergeant Jensen said as he revealed to Tim that investigators had tracked the locations of Colleen's and Tim's phones in addition to the Dodge Ram's cellular data.

The detectives worked to determine at what point in the day Tim switched vehicles with Colleen, confronting him with the location data. When Tim admitted using the truck to run a couple of errands midday, the investigators revealed they had surveillance photos of the Dodge Ram with no license plate and without the Superman decals that Tim claimed proved his innocence. Tim refused to acknowledge the evidence and continued to insist that if his truck was involved in the crime, Colleen wasn't the one driving it.

"Who do you think took your truck from your house and went to shoot Nicole?" Sergeant Jensen said, emphasizing the absurdity of the conspiracy claim. "Who would have a reason to do that?"

"No one who lives at my house would have a reason to do that. Nicki works for you guys," Tim responded.

"Timothy, Timothy, Timothy, here's the deal. Your truck's there. It's a female suspect. It's not a robbery. It's not a carjacking. We have the incident on video, and there is an email," Sergeant Heyer said, revealing the incriminating email sent by Colleen before she left the Taekwondo studio.

"And here's what we're really worried about, and we need you to explain then if it's not the case: you somehow conspired with Colleen to do this. You have a rock-solid alibi. Think about it. You've got a perfect alibi. You're sitting right there inside the business," Sergeant Jensen said.

Tim continued to deny any involvement and did not show any interest in implicating Colleen. He began his familiar loop of grievances concerning Nicki and the family court system, but this time with a softened edge, portraying himself as virtuous and with a simple goal of shining light on corruption. Tim went as far as to claim, "I haven't had any issues with that girl."

"Nicole? Sounds like it's been about five years of hell!" the skeptical detective shot back.

"And it's sad what happened to her," Tim replied. "To be honest with you guys, taking somebody's life or shooting somebody or hurting somebody does not bring justice into a situation, period. In fact, it's the easy way out. Taking a person out back and shooting them in the back of the head—that's the easy way out. That does nothing for anybody in the situation."

"You had nothing to do with conspiring or telling Colleen to commit this crime?" Sergeant Heyer asked.

"No, no, no," Tim repeated.

"So, her committing this crime would be completely on her own?" Sergeant Heyer followed up.

"I don't think she committed it," Tim maintained.

The detectives then pivoted to ask Tim how many guns he owned.

"I don't know," Tim said.

"Come on, man, really?" Sergeant Heyer asked in disbelief.

Tim then admitted he owned six guns. As he listed the various calibers of the firearms, pausing frequently and thinking aloud, Tim made another extremely incriminating omission.

"I noticed you didn't mention a .380 in there," Sgt. Jensen pointed out.

The spent shell casings and the live ammo found at the crime scene were .380 ammo, and as the interrogation was taking place, other investigators were searching Tim's home, trying to find the gun used in the attempt to kill Nicki. Tim responded that he used to have two .380 handguns, but he said that he had gotten rid of both of them. One, he sold to a well-known prosecutor who helped convict Derek Chauvin for the murder of George Floyd. Tim claimed he had given the other to Nicki for self-protection when she feared for her safety after committing "evidence tampering."

The scenario Tim implied with the latter claim was ludicrous—the possibility that a shooter somehow stole from Nicki a .380 handgun that once belonged to Tim and then used it in an attempt to murder her in public. The detectives were far beyond believing anything Tim said. Over the course of the fifty-six-minute interview, they showed him a lot of evidence and pointed out how his explanations didn't make sense.

Sergeant Jensen and Sergeant Heyer told Tim that Colleen was in the next interview room and that they needed to go speak with her and see how her story differed. After taking a DNA swab that Tim agreed to allow without a warrant, the detectives left Tim alone in the room for another ninety-five minutes.

At that point, the two lead detectives sent Sergeant Marcus Benner into the room. Tim remembered him from the night of the shooting when he asked Tim if his Jeep was his only vehicle. While Sergeant Jensen and Sergeant Heyer certainly were not easy on Tim, Sergeant Benner took an even harsher tone.

"I think you and I know you were being deceitful about it," Sergeant Benner said, revealing that he already knew Tim had a black Dodge Ram when he asked the question. "You know damn well I was interested in that truck."

When Tim tried to interrupt Sergeant Benner's questions and take control of the conversation, the detective stopped him. When Tim looked away, Benner redirected his attention and demanded eye contact.

"Look here. I'm asking you very simple questions. And you know that I'm asking you simple questions," Sergeant Benner said. "I want you to grasp the bigger picture—this shit you're in right now."

"But I didn't fucking do shit, and I understand that Nicki wants to do anything that she can to pinch it on me like she always has," Tim said.

"Let's stop. If there was an explanation, today was when you explain it. I don't feel like it was explained," Sergeant Benner said. "Dude, it's either a little bit of time away from your son or a long time. You got caught. You went sloppy; you got caught."

As Sergeant Jensen and Sergeant Heyer reentered the room and handcuffed Tim, telling him he would be going to jail on suspicion of conspiracy to commit murder, Tim made one final defiant statement.

"It doesn't even matter at this point," Tim said. "You guys are doing everything in your power to help out your coworker."

CHAPTER THIRTY-ONE

As Senior Assistant Hennepin County Attorney Patrick Lofton prepared charges against Tim and Colleen, he reviewed the new evidence collected by investigators who searched their house, the Taekwondo studio, and surveillance video from both locations. Police did not find the weapon used to shoot Nicki or any other .380 handgun. They did, however, find an empty hard plastic gun case clearly labeled for a Sig Sauer P238 .380 caliber pistol. They also found an ammunition magazine for a .380, along with discharged .380 cartridge casings at Tim's home.

The Hennepin County Crime Lab, which had taken over the processing of evidence in this case from Nicki's coworkers at the Minneapolis Crime Lab to avoid a conflict of interest, inspected the spent casings. The crime scene investigators determined the casings found at Tim and Colleen's home were likely fired by the same gun used to shoot Nicki.

Besides the gun, there was another key piece of evidence notably missing from Tim's house. While he was being interrogated by the lead detectives on the case, Tim repeatedly pointed out he had surveillance cameras at his home and that he'd be willing to show them the video that proved his and Colleen's innocence. However, when the detectives executing the search warrants obtained the footage taken by the Blink cameras, two key clips were missing. Videos timestamped at 7:13 p.m. and 7:40 p.m., which would have been the clips showing Colleen leaving with the Dodge Ram then returning after the shooting, were deleted from the cloud. In addition, a DVR hooked up to other cameras installed on the home had no video on it at all. Like many conspiracy cases, it appeared the absence or cover-up of evidence was just as important as the evidence that could be recovered.

Video collected from the studio seemingly answered another question. Although the view is partially obstructed, one camera captured Tim doing something on the side of the Dodge Ram truck the morning after the shooting. It appeared likely that he was applying the Superman decals that he claimed were on the truck the whole time. On the video, when the truck drove in, the decals could not be seen. When the truck drove out, there was the "S" on the side panel in front of the rear-view mirror.

After word started spreading that Tim and Colleen were jailed with a thirty-six-hour hold ticking down until charges would need to be filed, some of Tim's friends and former associates began to come forward with disturbing new details. In the months prior to the shooting, just weeks after the judge ordered the return to supervised visitation, Tim was spiraling with his drinking. During that period, Tim frequently told dark jokes while drunk about needing to find a way to "get rid" of Nicki or make her "go away."

One of Tim's friends came forward with a darker story that he heard second-hand and no longer took as a joke in light of what happened. A mutual friend of Tim's told him weeks before the shooting that Tim had propositioned him to kill Nicki in exchange for $50,000. The would-be hitman turned Tim down. A second-hand story like that cannot be used in court, so police were determined to get it directly from the person Tim propositioned. Police corroborated the conversation through phone and text records. When a detective reached the would-be hitman, however, he denied it—sounding afraid and concerned about Tim's possible release from jail.

Tim's neighbor, Charlie Dettloff, who had known him his entire adult life, was devastated when he heard the news about the shooting. The initial circumstances sounded pretty damning to him even though Tim hadn't been arrested and charged yet during the first week that followed. Charlie invited Tim over for a cigar and a glass of whiskey, something they had done countless times together while they were next-door neighbors.

Charlie fully expected that at some point during the conversation, even if not right away, Tim would say something to the effect of, "Oh my God, did you hear what happened to Nicki?" Charlie's plan was to let Tim bring it up, then feel out whether to directly ask him if he was involved. Charlie thought it was possible Tim would confide in him about it, unprompted.

To Charlie's surprise, Tim never even mentioned the shooting. Over the course of two hours, as they sat on Charlie's back porch, Tim talked about his mother, his brother's substance abuse issues, his friend's children, essentially everything except the shooting of the mother of his child and the news reports concerning it that everyone had seen by then.

When the cigars burned out, and the liquor was gone, the conversation wrapped up just like it always did. Charlie suggested they hang out in Tim's hot tub sometime in the coming week or catch dinner—just leaving the door open to talk again. By failing to acknowledge the enormous elephant in the room, Tim just as well could have confessed to Charlie. The neighbor knew his long-time friend was involved, and nothing would be the same after that.

Every one of Tim's neighbors and friends who agreed to talk to the police characterized Tim and Colleen's relationship the same way—unequal, with "Master Amacher" maintaining all the power, and Colleen willfully subservient. Several of them didn't believe Colleen had it in her to wield a gun, let alone fire it, but the lead detectives discovered that Colleen was actually formally trained to carry and fire a gun. She applied for her concealed carry permit fifteen months before the shooting and took her class from another Taekwondo master, James Franklin. Master Franklin told police he had heard all about Tim's frustrations with his custody battle.

In putting together the charges, it was important for the prosecutor to find the most serious crime possible that fit the actions Tim and Colleen each took. For Colleen, first-degree attempted murder was an easy conclusion to reach because there was evidence she intended to kill Nicki as part of a premeditated plot. For Tim, Patrick thought it would be easy to prove the charge of aiding an offender after the fact. Tim's omission that he had a black Dodge Ram truck and leaving out the .380 handgun from his list of weapons, along with the deleted home surveillance video, all constituted evidence of misdirection after the shooting.

Patrick firmly believed that charge alone was not serious enough for Tim's role in the crime, so he also charged Tim with aiding and abetting first-degree attempted murder. In Minnesota, if someone is convicted of aiding and abetting murder or attempted murder, the penalties are just as severe as for the person who pulled the trigger. Patrick would need to prove that Tim recruited Colleen to shoot Nicki—that he was the mastermind behind the crime.

Tim unwittingly provided some evidence of premeditation during his interview with the two lead detectives. He revealed that the day before the shooting, he went to the motor vehicle office to order new vanity license plates. He told police his previous plates had been stolen, which turned out to be a lie. Patrick's theory was that Tim knew Colleen couldn't drive to the shooting scene with plates on the truck because the chance of being identified would be too high. But if she got pulled over on the way there without a plate, she would then have an excuse as to why. It would have to be the world's biggest coincidence for Tim to have set up the truck without a license plate the day before the shooting, for Colleen to have used the same vehicle for the shooting without his knowledge, and for Tim to omit possession of such a truck until confronted with evidence from police. It seemed clear that Tim planned the shooting and that he just didn't count on police tracking the truck.

The long history between Tim and Nicki and then the timing of the return to supervised visits pointed to only one conclusion. Patrick didn't have one particular bit of evidence that proved the case, but all the pieces of circumstantial evidence, plus the motive, all pointed back to Tim. On May 2, 2022, Patrick filed the charges that would keep Tim in jail until his trial.

CHAPTER THIRTY-TWO

Nicki was elated when she learned Tim and Colleen were arrested. She was with her parents and Donovan when she got the news. She was still hospitalized, and it happened the same day she saw Callahan for the first time since the shooting.

Over the first eight days of Nicki's hospitalization, her parents had cared for Cal and conveyed some information about his mom's condition to the five-year-old. When Nicki could whisper slightly, they let Cal talk with her on the phone. Finally, on day eight, Nicki's charge nurse told her, "You need to see your kid," and she allowed the visit even though children visitors were not allowed in the surgical intensive care unit (SICU) where Nicki was being treated.

Nicki's dad, Joe, brought Cal to her room. He tentatively walked in, scared of the feeding tube and IVs coming out of Nicki, along with her bandaged bullet wounds. Cal walked to the edge of the bed.

"It's OK. I'm OK. Come here," Nicki whispered, patting the bed next to her.

She could tell her son just didn't know how to interact with her in that state. Nicki started explaining how the feeding tube worked and what the other equipment in the hospital room was for. At that point, in addition to telling Cal that his mom had fallen, Nicki's parents explained that someone else had caused her injuries. However, he didn't know that she had been shot.

"So, you fell on your neck?" he asked his mom, pointing at the bandage covering her near-fatal gunshot wound.

"Well, kind of," Nicki replied in a raspy whisper.

"You broke your arm, too?" Cal asked.

"Yes, that's right," Nicki responded.

"You sound so funny. You don't sound like my mom," Cal said multiple times as he started to get more comfortable in this first interaction.

"I know. I might have a funny voice from now on, but at least I can talk," Nicki explained to her son.

Their visit ended with Nicki telling Cal how proud she was that he was being so good for Grandma and Grandpa and how well he was doing at school.

"I love you, and before you know it, I'll be out of the hospital and home, and we will be together again," Nicki said as they hugged and said goodbye.

The fifteen-minute impromptu visit with her son eased Nicki's mind more than any development in the case could have, but she had a lot to monitor in court as well. Despite the prosecution initially requesting a $1 million bail amount for Tim, the judge set it at $750,000 or $250,000 if he agreed to follow the conditions of the court. That meant if he paid a bail bond company 10 percent of that, or $25,000, he could be released until his trial.

The judge agreed to raise the amount, however, after learning about suspicious phone calls Tim had made from jail. One call sounded to investigators as if his best friend Dimitris Kelly had informed Tim that two of their friends had reported the $50,000 offer for a hit on Nicki.

"Slim and Patrick went to police and told them, uh..." Dimitris began. "Told them what we discussed. Slim and Patrick went to the police and told them that. The police said that was hearsay, and they don't need that information anyway. Then they had Slim and Patrick call that other person, and that other person said, 'Nah man, we were drinking, but we were just talking, and that's all it was. It wasn't even about that.' And so that what they told the po', and so just letting you know that."

"What does Patrick have to do with anything?" Tim asked, which police believed referred to the fact that Tim's longtime friend and former roommate Patrick Zellmer was reporting information he heard second-hand.

"That's what I fucking wonder!" Dimitris responded. "Slim and Patrick have been running back and forth talkin', running their mouth about stuff they know nothing about! Trying to be the judge, the jury."

Police and prosecutors believed the jail phone conversation gave credibility to the claim Tim was willing to pay someone to kill Nicki prior to Colleen's attempt. Senior Assistant County Attorney Patrick Lofton convinced the judge it was evidence of how dangerous Tim could be if released from jail, so the judge raised Tim's bail to $1 million.

When the criminal charges were filed, including a probable cause statement laying out some of the evidence against Tim and Colleen, it was the first time Nicki had heard many of those details from the investigation. Besides the criminal case, Nicki needed to take additional steps to protect herself and her son. Her family court attorney, Stacy Lofgren, filed a modification request to the custody case to immediately suspend Tim's parenting time to ensure that if he were released, Tim would have no legal visitation or access to Callahan.

In addition, before Tim and Colleen were charged, Nicki filed an order for protection for herself and on behalf of Cal to add a layer of safety in case Tim was free without any other court order to stay away. Even though Stacy could have appeared in the virtual hearing on Nicki's behalf, Nicki wanted to do it herself. She attended the virtual hearing with her camera turned on so that Tim could see she was alive and well, and so the judge could see the wound to her neck and fully grasp the danger Tim posed. However, Tim ended up not logging onto the hearing, asking his attorney to handle it for him alone instead.

Referee Elizabeth Clysdale, who had ordered the return to supervised visitation for Tim three months earlier, signed every order on behalf of Nicki and Cal, showing empathy and promising to do as much for them as the law would allow.

After ten days in the hospital, Nicki was discharged to continue her recovery at home. She and Cal moved into Donovan's home with plans to prepare her house for sale. On Memorial Day 2022, Donovan and Rae planned a celebration of Nicki's survival.

Family, friends, and coworkers at the Minneapolis Police Department got together at a suburban park on a warm day. While most of the dozens of guests were gathered under the park shelter, Donovan—who is introverted—announced for everyone to listen up.

"I want to thank everyone for being here," Donovan said, his arm around Nicki, who looked like herself aside from a scar on her neck and her broken arm still in a cast. "We're all here for her—everybody pretty much knows what happened and her miraculous recovery."

The guests began a round of applause as Nicki smiled at Donovan. He then continued.

"I especially want to thank my boys who showed up at the hospital the night it happened. Those guys who showed up at the hospital to be her security, it means a lot," Donovan said, addressing his fellow officers who were there at the park with their families continuing to show support.

Donovan shifted to Nicki's other side and reached his left hand into the pocket of his shorts.

"I'm not a public speaker; I'm not good at all that stuff. With all friends and family here, I thought it fitting if I do this here, so," Donovan said as he looked to Nicki, pulled a white box out of his pocket, and got down on one knee.

"Miss Nicole Lenway, will you marry me?" Donovan asked as the crowd squealed.

Nicki nodded emphatically, her hand to her face in shock. Guests clapped and cheered, so touched by the moment that had come after weeks of hoping and praying for Nicki's full recovery. As Donovan stood up, Nicki kissed him, and they hugged. She had found the man who loved her and treated her the way she deserved, and she never wanted to let him go.

Nicki and Donovan. Photo furnished by Nicki Lenway.

CHAPTER THIRTY-THREE

Three weeks after she was arrested and denied any involvement in the shooting of Nicki Lenway, Colleen Larson began to change her story. Colleen's attorney, Dan Adkins, reached out to prosecutors about the possibility of a proffer.

A proffer is a statement or interview given to authorities with the agreement that it cannot be used against the defendant in their case. It is common in aiding and abetting cases where prosecutors want to ensure a conviction against the main culprit and are willing to cut deals with accomplices in order to make that happen.

What made Colleen's case unique is that she was the shooter—the principal actor in the crime—while Tim was the one who "aided and abetted." Yet, ensuring a conviction against Tim was everyone's highest priority because they knew Colleen would never have done anything without Tim's influence, and Tim would pose much more danger to Nicki in the future. Prosecutors wanted to know what information Colleen would be willing to share and if she would be reliable enough to testify against Tim in his trial. The benefit of the proffer is that they would not be locked into any sort of deal before the interview and could negotiate afterward. In addition, the process ensures that the defendant cannot simply tell prosecutors whatever they think will secure a good plea deal.

On May 24, 2022, lead detectives Sergeant Michael Heyer and Sergeant James Jensen, along with Senior Assistant County Attorney Patrick Lofton, walked into an interview room where Colleen and her two attorneys waited.

"You hopefully understand the purpose of this is to come and get your story because we didn't think we got your story originally," Sergeant Jensen said. "Does that make sense? The only thing that can hurt you in all this is if you're not truthful."

As Colleen began talking, the prosecutor and two investigators at first thought she was going to spill all the details.

"I took the truck; I drove over there. I parked it up on the hill. Then, I waited for the female. Then I ran up and shot her," Colleen calmly and quietly recited, noticeably avoiding Nicki's name.

Colleen shared that she changed clothes in the backseat of the truck to hide her identity—something she learned from crime shows. When asked by Sergeant Jensen whether Tim had suggested she wear a disguise, Colleen's voice raised an octave, and it then became apparent she would not be as cooperative as investigators had hoped. Sounding like a child forced by an adult to tattle on their friend, Colleen answered questions about Tim in a quiet whine.

"Tell us about those conversations," Sergeant Jensen said.

"I don't really know how to describe it," Colleen whined.

"OK, well, let me back you up for a second," Sergeant Jensen said, sounding a bit impatient. "Whose idea was it to shoot Nicole?"

"Tim's," Colleen said after a long pause.

"And how did that come about?" Sergeant Jensen asked.

"Because he didn't think the justice system was being very just," Colleen cryptically answered.

Giving one- or two-word answers to each of the detective's follow-up questions, Colleen eventually acknowledged she had a conversation with Tim about a week or two before the shooting. In that conversation, Colleen claimed Tim asked her whether she would "feel comfortable" pulling the trigger.

"What were his words?" Patrick asked, knowing vague answers wouldn't work with a jury if he called Colleen as a witness. "Say what he said to you."

"I can't tell you because I don't remember," Colleen answered. "I pretty much just…I don't remember, honestly."

Sergeant Heyer cut to the heart of what he believed Tim must have told her.

"Did he talk about how he would be inside with his child and witnesses being there, which would keep him safe because he might be the number one suspect with all his issues with Nicole? Was that discussed with you? And why you would be better at committing this than him?" Sergeant Heyer asked.

"Kind of," Colleen answered in a sing-song whine.

"Do you remember how he talked about that?" Sergeant Heyer followed up.

When Colleen didn't answer, Sergeant Jensen let out a frustrated sigh and told Colleen they needed her to be completely honest. He pointed out that they could all tell she was holding back. Even Colleen's attorney, Dan Adkins, tried encouraging her.

"I've heard you tell me why and how this happened, and we all know why you don't want to tell the story," Dan said. "We need to own this, and we need to tell the whole story. They know you didn't cook this up. Why did this happen at this time and on this day, please?"

Colleen finally got a little more detailed in her answer. But rather than further implicate Tim with her answer, she seemed to be justifying her own actions.

"He asked me because he didn't feel like he was getting justice. He felt like the referee was being very racist and biased. I wanted to help out, but I didn't know how to help him out. I've tried different things, like calling CPS and sending emails. They didn't really seem to help. And I guess this is the only thing that I felt was left. And he kind of expressed that, too," Colleen said before disparaging Nicki. "I mean, I didn't like what she was doing, either. I didn't like her really all that much, either, and I wanted to help the little man. And when Tim asked me, I contemplated it."

"What did he ask? What did he say when he said this is the plan?" Dan asked his client.

"He just asked if I was comfortable with pulling the trigger," Colleen answered, returning to her original revelation while remaining vague on the details.

It was obvious to investigators that Colleen believed everything Tim had told her about Nicki. She genuinely believed Tim was the victim. At one point, Colleen referred to Nicki as Tim's "baby mama." She recited the same claims Tim made about Nicki abusing Callahan. When directly asked whether she believed Tim deserved to be charged in the shooting, Colleen said no. She didn't believe he deserved it, yet Colleen agreed she should face charges.

"I wanted to be his 'somebody' because he needed somebody in his corner. The world kept on beating on him. He kept on trying to do things the right way," Colleen said.

Eventually, in the hour and twenty-minute interview, in between pauses when Colleen broke down crying, she admitted Tim showed her where he kept a loaded gun in his bedroom drawer and how to operate the safety.

As Colleen sobbed, again recounting the shooting itself, detectives tried to determine how Colleen ended up spilling unspent rounds onto the ground. She didn't provide much insight besides acknowledging she was having trouble operating the gun.

"When you were standing over her and trying to shoot her, what were you thinking? Because she was still moving, were you trying to, I guess, kill her for sure? Make sure she's dead?" Sergeant Jensen asked.

"I was thinking, 'Why wasn't it firing?' I was like, 'Fuck!'" Colleen cried.

Colleen said she showered as soon as she got home and was already in bed when Tim finally got back after talking with the police. She claimed they did not talk about the shooting other than Tim saying he got home late because he was being investigated. Colleen had cut up the clothes she was wearing and put them in a bag with the gun, which she handed to Tim the next morning.

"He said he'd take care of it," Colleen told police without answering any questions about how exactly Tim knew what he was "taking care of."

Toward the end of the interview, Colleen revealed what sounded like her personal motive for taking part in the attempted murder plot—and likely the button Tim pushed to convince her to do it. Tim and Colleen had talked about marriage. She had asked him about adopting Cal, whom Colleen had babysat and grown to love in her own way since he was born. Tim told Colleen that would never happen as long as Nicki was around.

"But, like, 'If it's just you and me, then of course I'll let you adopt him,'" Colleen said Tim had told her just a week before the shooting.

During their six years living together, Colleen listened to Tim vent countless times about how he wanted to "get his family back together." Colleen seemed to believe that if Nicki were dead, she could replace her as Cal's mother and create the family Tim wanted. Knowing what they'd learned about Tim, the investigators didn't believe for a second that Tim intended to follow through with that plan. Once Nicki was out of the picture, he could leave Colleen and hold the murder over her head forever to make sure he was never implicated.

As the proffer interview ended, the detectives and especially the prosecutor were disappointed. There was no way Patrick could call Colleen as a witness. At best, she would confuse the jury about the clear evidence. At worst, she might try to completely take the fall for Tim. Patrick would have to prove Tim's guilt without the jury knowing that the shooter had admitted pulling the trigger.

CHAPTER

THIRTY-FOUR

Senior Assistant County Attorney Patrick Lofton teamed with Assistant County Attorney Jake Fischmann in preparing for Tim Amacher's trial scheduled to begin in November 2022. They split up the witnesses to prepare for with Jake planning the opening statement, and Patrick taking the closing argument. Their primary concern was that the jury wouldn't be able to see beyond the obvious evidence that Colleen was the shooter and agree that Tim set the plan in motion.

They had heard how Tim was able to convince people to see things his way: social worker Theresa Roberts, White Bear Lake prosecutor Luke McClure, and the workers at FamilyWise. Would he be able to convince jurors as well? The issue of race also loomed over the case. Tim had weaponized race against Nicki many times over the years. He hired a Black attorney, Larry Reed, to argue that Tim had been victimized over and over by the legal system in part because Tim was Black. In Minneapolis, so soon after the death of George Floyd and the race-fueled riots that followed, the two white prosecutors had no idea whether a Hennepin County jury would be sympathetic to Tim's claims.

Furthermore, the primary actor in a crime—in this case, the shooter—is typically the top suspect to be brought down. The prosecutors didn't want the jury to see Tim as a bit player in the attempted murder. That gave Jake an idea for a theme he and Patrick would weave throughout the case.

"Ladies and gentlemen, in this story, what the evidence is going to show is that while the defendant may not have been the actor that pulled the trigger," Jake told the jury in his opening statement, "He was the screenwriter, the director, and the producer."

Jake gave an overview of the chaotic relationship between Nicki and Tim, their attempt at co-parenting once Callahan was born, and Tim's descent into demented claims once Nicki started dating Donovan. While the norm at a criminal trial would be to avoid airing the victim's dirty laundry, Jake and Patrick wanted to get ahead of the smear campaign they knew would be coming from Tim's defense. They previewed the false claims Tim made to police and CPS and how his jealousy grew throughout the custody battle.

"It gets to the point that one of the leading child abuse doctors in the state of Minnesota directs law enforcement not to submit any more cases to their office because it's not the abuse of the child by Ms. Lenway that he's concerned about; it's the abuse of the child by the defendant in bringing the child into all these bogus allegations. And you're going to hear evidence that this leads the courts to say, 'Look, your visitation with Callahan has got to be supervised,'" Jake told the jury.

Jake then segued into telling the jury about FamilyWise, about Colleen Larson, and about the shooting itself. He previewed the location data and surveillance video evidence that would prove Colleen was the shooter along with the interactions with Tim afterward that proved he was behind it.

"I want you to pay close attention to what he says, how he says it, what he does, his affect, his demeanor, and I'll give you a preview. The evidence is going to show that officers say, 'The mother of your child was just shot in the parking lot while you were sitting inside.' And Tim responds, 'This is all a setup by the Minneapolis Police Department to get me in trouble.' I'll leave it to you to figure out if that's an appropriate reaction to finding this out or if this shows that Mr. Amacher knew what was going on," Jake said.

After previewing the evidence, Jake reminded the jury, "Ladies and gentlemen, the evidence is going to show in this case that while the defendant was not the shooter, he pressed the play button. The evidence is going to show that he was the screenwriter for how this was going to go down; he was the director for how it went the day of; and he was the producer, providing everything that was needed for the crime. Ladies and gentlemen, the evidence is going to show that the defendant is guilty of attempted murder."

As Tim sat at the defense table in a dark suit, the bottom half of his face covered by a medical mask, his attorney, Larry Reed, addressed the jury, telling them his client was wrongfully accused and did nothing. As expected, Larry quickly got extremely specific about alleged injuries Tim found on Callahan—a black eye, a burned hand, bruises all over his body, a bruised penis, and a lacerated penis.

"What is he supposed to do?" Larry rhetorically asked the jury. "He made a report."

Larry told the jury that Tim had reported Nicki to internal affairs and provided them with a tape-recorded conversation showing that Nicki fabricated evidence in the Jamar Clark case. It was the first time the public had heard the explosive accusation stated openly, and the defense attorney had to know exactly how it would land. The police shooting of Jamar Clark remained a controversial case in many circles in Minneapolis, and here, in front of a jury, a defense attorney was insinuating that the jury would hear a recording that proved Nicki had fabricated evidence. The Minnesota Bureau of Criminal Apprehension took note and would later interview Nicki about the claim. Even while standing trial for attempting to murder her, Tim somehow managed to upend Nicki's life and reputation with another false allegation.

As he continued his opening statement, Larry offered the jury an alternative analysis of Tim's actions and statements to police after the shooting. He told them Tim did express concern for Nicki's well-being and tried to cooperate with the police.

Then, he told the jury that the black truck they would see in images throughout the trial was actually not Tim's Dodge Ram. Larry previewed the same discrepancies Tim tried to claim, such as the Superman decal and GT emblem and told the jury that the color of the truck itself didn't match.

Larry implied that Colleen wasn't actually the shooter, that IMSI location data evidence is not reliable, and that the one hundred potential witnesses on the prosecution's list were there just to make up for the fact none of them could prove Tim did anything.

"This stuff about directing and producing, I guess, a movie or something really is not what this case is about," Larry said. "The question is about evidence. We've got to defend all this other stuff, which puts us in a difficult position, but we're here to do it, and we will ask the appropriate questions."

CHAPTER THIRTY-FIVE

For a trial with details as salacious as this, one might expect courtroom observers to find the testimony captivating. However, defense attorney Larry Reed managed to make the proceedings nearly unwatchable throughout many stretches by objecting to nearly every question asked and forcing Judge Shereen Askalani to remind him dozens of times to speak into his microphone when she couldn't hear anything Larry said.

Juror Laura Sweeney immediately started to wonder whether he was coming to court unprepared or if it was an intentional tactic to delay and stretch out the trial as much as possible. The rest of the jury felt the same, even eventually letting Judge Askalani's clerk know they were frustrated. The judge admonished Larry, repeatedly telling him that the jury couldn't hear or understand him and that they couldn't hear what witnesses or the prosecutors were saying when Larry would talk over them.

Testimony progressed through several emotional witnesses, such as Megan Curran, who witnessed the shooting at

FamilyWise, and Emilie Clancie, who heroically helped Nicki until police and EMS arrived. They described what the jury was seeing on police body camera video in the immediate aftermath.

The jury was captivated by the testimony of FBI Special Agent Richard Fennern, who was a national asset with the FBI's Cellular Analysis Survey Team. His specialty was analyzing and then simplifying cellular location data for the jury's benefit. Through a series of maps, he showed the jury the path traveled throughout the day of the shooting by Tim's phone, Colleen's phone, and the Dodge Ram truck—which he instructed the jury to visualize as a large cell phone itself.

In the jury box, Laura could see the steps Tim took to try to outsmart the technology. He clearly did not take into consideration that the truck could be tracked, she thought. Larry's attempts in cross-examination to diminish that evidence and even suggest the truck shown to the jury was different fell flat. One damning video from the day of the shooting showed Tim driving the Dodge Ram through a KFC drive thru. The footage revealed plainly that there were no license plates on the truck and no Superman decals on the front fenders or doors while Tim was behind the wheel.

After Tim's misdirection concerning his ownership of a .380 handgun, the same caliber used to shoot Nicki, prosecutors were forced to call Twin Cities attorney Steve Schleicher to testify. When the lead detectives confronted Tim about his omission of the .380, Tim claimed he had owned two of them at different times, selling one of them to Schleicher and giving the other one to Nicki. Schleicher was well-known in Minnesota at the time of the 2022 trial because one year earlier, he was part of the team that convicted former MPD Officer Derek Chauvin of murdering George Floyd.

On the witness stand, Schleicher testified credibly that he had worked out at Tim's gym, his children took Taekwondo classes from him, and—about eight to ten years earlier—Tim had sold him a Ruger .380 caliber handgun. With Schleicher's testimony showing that the Ruger .380 was out of Tim's possession for several years, that meant the Sig Sauer .380 that matched the plastic case investigators found in Tim's house was still unaccounted for. Patrick would address that missing weapon when Nicki took the stand the next day.

Although Colleen was not on trial together with Tim, prosecutors needed the jury to believe she was the shooter in order to convict Tim of aiding and abetting in the plot to try to murder Nicki. After Colleen conducted the proffer interview in late May, her family helped her bail out of jail while she awaited resolution in her criminal case. The judge gave the Larsons permission to go to the Saint Paul home she shared with Tim and gather her belongings. After she and Tim had been arrested, next-door neighbor Charlie Dettloff was given the keys to the duplex to hold onto until further notice.

Charlie already had strong feelings about Tim's role in crime. He had known the man his entire adult life, and it was extremely telling that during the long conversation they had in the days following the shooting, Tim never mentioned that the mother of his son was fighting for her life in the hospital.

After that, Charlie went to the courthouse to further his own research. There, he read through the dozens of motions to the court and reports to police and CPS—false claims made by Tim once Nicki no longer wanted to date him. Charlie felt embarrassed that in the middle of the custody battle, he was one of the dozens of friends and acquaintances who wrote a letter of support for Tim to help his chances for a favorable custody ruling.

With visits from investigating officers and his conversation with Tim still fresh in his mind, Charlie received notice in Summer 2022 that he needed to unlock Tim's duplex for Colleen to retrieve her belongings. She arrived with her father and brother, who helped her carry out her things. Over the six years that Colleen had lived there, Charlie had a few occasional conversations with Colleen's dad, whom he found friendly and genuine.

As Charlie stood awkwardly in the entryway monitoring the move-out, Colleen began to cry. She ran up to Charlie and gave him a huge hug, sobbing.

"I did this. I pulled the trigger," Colleen cried to Charlie. "This is all my fault. Will you write me if I go to prison?"

Charlie hugged Colleen back, shocked by the interaction. He locked eyes with Colleen's dad—who looked equally surprised and deflated by the realization that Colleen had just made Charlie a witness to a confession for the attempted murder of Nicki Lenway.

"Colleen, you can't. You can't talk," Charlie told her.

When Charlie took the witness stand in Tim's trial, prosecutor Patrick Lofton built up the beginning of Charlie's testimony with his twenty-year history with Tim, not just as a neighbor but as a close friend. Charlie testified about his observations of Tim's relationship with Nicki as well as his relationship with Colleen. He detailed the suspicious conversation with Tim after the shooting and built up to the confession from Colleen amid incessant objections from Larry, which Judge Askalani overruled.

"She ran toward you, and what happened?" Patrick asked.

"She came at me, she hugged me, and she said that she pulled the trigger," Charlie testified.

"No further questions," Patrick said.

CHAPTER THIRTY-SIX

On the sixth day of testimony in Tim's attempted murder trial, the jury saw the victim in person for the very first time. Judge Shereen Askalani had ordered Nicki—like all witnesses—to be sequestered during the trial, meaning she wasn't allowed to watch other witnesses testify so that their testimony would not influence hers. During her trial preparation with prosecutors Patrick Lofton and Jake Fischmann, they developed a plan for a bit of a surprise at the beginning of her testimony.

The jury watched Nicki walk into the courtroom with confidence, successfully hiding any nerves she felt. After Nicki was sworn in and identified Tim in the courtroom as the father of her child, Patrick proceeded with his questions.

"Are you married?" Patrick asked.

"Yes, I am," Nicki answered, glancing over to Tim at the defendant's table.

Above his mask, she saw Tim's eyes get big, as she saw them do countless times when he got angry during their relationship.

He had no idea she and Donovan had gotten married less than one month before the trial.

"Is it some big secret that you guys are together?" Patrick asked, getting ahead of Tim's lies and insinuations that Nicki was dating several different cops.

"No, it's not," Nicki said.

"Do all of your colleagues know that y'all are married?" Patrick asked.

"Yes, they do," Nicki said.

Although her friends, family, and coworkers were all aware of the marriage, no one in the court case had mentioned it publicly until Nicki broke the news while under oath. She explained that she was currently working on the legal name change to become Nicole Ford.

"If someone claims that you changed your name due to some controversy on a case that you worked on in 2015, is that true?" Patrick asked, subtly reminding the jury about one of the many claims Tim made in his police interview.

"No," Nicki said.

"Did you ever tamper with evidence in the Jamar Clark case?" Patrick asked.

"No," Nicki said.

"Did you ever tamper with evidence in any case?" Patrick asked.

"No," Nicki said.

Patrick made some effort to show the jury the difference between Nicki's role as a civilian forensic scientist and the sworn officers at the Minneapolis Police Department. She didn't carry a gun while at work, and she testified that she didn't carry a gun for personal protection either. Patrick was building toward Tim's claim that the .380 gun missing from the empty Sig Sauer case in his house had been given to the victim years before the crime.

"Did the defendant ever give you a .380 handgun?" Patrick asked.

"No," Nicki said.

"Have you ever owned a .380 handgun?" Patrick asked.

"I've never owned any gun," Nicki said.

Throughout the entire day she spent on the witness stand, Patrick asked Nicki a great deal about the history of her relationship with Tim—his alcohol abuse, jealousy, and anger.

"He would be fine when we'd be out with his friends, but we would get home, and something I said or did would make him fly into a rage. And he would scream at me and corner me. I would try to close myself in a different room or whatever to get away from the situation and try to disengage. And he would just follow me around the house and berate me," Nicki testified.

The jury looked intently at Nicki as she described several specific nightmarish encounters. Juror Laura Sweeney thought to herself how humiliating it must be for Nicki to have to lay her whole life in front of them like that in such graphic detail. She admired Nicki for having the courage to do it, knowing it was needed in order to help the jury see Tim's motive for wanting to kill her.

One of the most impactful parts of Nicki's testimony came when she told the story of Tim's false accusation that she ran over his foot. The jury looked over to Tim's defense table and envisioned the inverse situation—Nicki sitting at the defense table while a prosecutor accused her of intentionally striking down Tim and her toddler son with her SUV.

"Did you testify in that trial?" Patrick asked.

"Yes, I did," Nicki answered.

"Did Mr. Amacher testify in that trial?" Patrick asked.

"Yes, he did," Nicki answered.

"How long did the jury deliberate?" Patrick asked.

"Five minutes," Nicki answered.

Laura and the other jurors listening knew that in a matter of days they would be deliberating Tim's fate. Learning that a similar panel of twelve took just minutes to clear Nicki after hearing her version and Tim's version spoke volumes to the jury about Nicki's credibility.

As her testimony neared the mid-morning break, Nicki looked out at the spectators seated in the courtroom gallery. A short, middle-aged Black woman seated toward the back—behind Tim's table—caught her attention. It was Theresa Roberts, the Dakota County social worker who made Nicki's life hell while she awaited the judge's ruling in the custody case.

After the jury was out of the courtroom, Nicki notified her victim advocate, who messaged Patrick, who wasted no time bringing the violation to the judge's attention.

"Are you Theresa Roberts?" Patrick called out.

"Yes," she answered.

Judge Askalani was astonished. "Go take a seat in the hallway," she instructed Theresa.

None of the case's potential witnesses were supposed to be in the courtroom, and here, during the most anticipated testimony of the whole trial, one of Tim's witnesses—who was on the short list of people who believed him over Nicki—was there in violation of the judge's order.

Defense attorney Larry Reed insisted to the judge that he had no idea Theresa was in the courtroom. Larry claimed his investigator had served Theresa her subpoena to testify and that she never followed the instructions to reach out to them. Judge Askalani told Larry she found it "interesting" that Theresa would randomly show up during Nicki's testimony—not during body camera footage, not during the cell phone evidence—just when Nicki, whom Theresa refused to believe, was on the witness stand. Among Minnesotans, the word "interesting" carries several different meanings, in this case—"suspicious."

After the mid-morning break ended, and the jury was back in the courtroom, Patrick found a way to use the frustrating development to their advantage. He asked Nicki under oath about Theresa Roberts, and she explained that Theresa was a Dakota County social worker.

"Why does she stick out in your mind amongst the social workers that you dealt with?" Patrick asked.

"She basically, from the beginning, was accusing me of abusing Callahan. And regardless of what I said to her or tried to convey to her, she told me she was going to try to take Callahan because she didn't feel he was safe with me," Nicki answered.

Nicki testified that none of the other child protection professionals she was forced to deal with treated her that way.

"Did you see Theresa Roberts sitting in the courtroom here earlier?" Patrick asked.

"Yes, I did," Nicki answered.

"How did that make you feel?" Patrick asked.

"Objection, your honor, irrelevant!" Larry interjected.

"Overruled. You may answer," Judge Askalani said.

"Concerned," Nicki answered. "I feel like, as a social worker, you should be unbiased in the work, and clearly, she came in support of Tim. So, I don't know why she would come, I guess, to this type of hearing."

For extra emphasis and in case Larry still intended to call Theresa as a witness, Patrick asked Nicki one final question about the social worker to destroy her credibility.

"Was Theresa Roberts eventually instructed not to work on your case?" Patrick asked.

"Yes," Nicki answered.

CHAPTER THIRTY-SEVEN

Several members of the jury were parents themselves and had dealt with the ordinary bumps and bruises that young children—particularly energetic little boys—suffer throughout childhood. They listened with understanding as prosecutor Patrick Lofton went through with Nicki each alleged injury defense attorney Larry Reed had alluded to in his opening statement and cross-examination of other witnesses. At that point in the trial, jurors had lost count of how many times they heard Larry use the phrase "lacerated penis."

"Have you ever punished your son by trying to hurt his penis?" Patrick asked.

"No," Nicki said.

"Is that kind of a disgusting question to even have to be asked?" Patrick followed up.

"Yes," Nicki agreed.

Larry attempted to object to what everyone in the courtroom knew was a subtle knock on his and Tim's defense, but

Judge Askalani overruled him. Patrick and Nicki also pointed out that family court Referee Elizabeth Clysdale had already heard all of those child abuse allegations and still gave Nicki full legal and physical custody.

After thoroughly priming the jury with hours of testimony about the hell Tim put Nicki through, Patrick began asking her about the shooting itself. She recounted the captivating details of the incident that nearly took her life, then showed the jury her permanent scars and lasting effects.

"Are you a person who likes to sing?" Patrick asked.

"I am," Nicki replied.

"Can you sing anymore?"

"No," Nicki answered. "From the damage to my vocal cords, I don't have the strength. It still hasn't completely healed. They don't know if it ever will. But at this point, I'm just lucky to be alive and happy that I can talk. We didn't know if I'd ever be able to talk again."

Nicki finished her testimony by telling the jury she had never received threats from anyone else regarding her work in the Minneapolis Police Department or in her personal life.

As he began his cross-examination, Larry attempted to poke holes in Nicki's testimony by re-characterizing her relationship with Tim in the ways Tim had described it to others—that they dated essentially until the time Nicki started dating Donovan. Nicki firmly rejected that notion. When Larry began noting specific reports of abuse, things Callahan allegedly said, Patrick successfully objected to hearsay.

Some jurors began to cringe as Larry repeatedly questioned Nicki about Cal's "lacerated penis." Larry defended the fact Tim took Cal to urgent care appointments despite Nicki's steady answers that she was in charge of medical decisions for their son as stated in the custody ruling.

The cross-examination built to a crescendo with questions about the Minneapolis Police shooting of Jamar Clark. Larry wanted to leave the jury with the possibility that someone upset with the outcome of that case had a motive to shoot Nicki in the FamilyWise parking lot. Nicki repeated that she had not done any DNA testing in that case and had nothing to do with its outcome.

When Larry finished, Patrick had one more turn to question Nicki based on the issues Larry raised about the Jamar Clark case.

"How does it feel to be accused of that in a public courtroom?" Patrick asked.

"It's embarrassing. This is my career that I worked really hard to get, and it feels like just another way he's trying to undermine my future and harass me and hurt me," Nicki said.

After Nicki finished her testimony, she exited the courtroom still under the sequestration order in case prosecutors needed to call her as a rebuttal witness following Tim's testimony. In the jury box, Laura was very impressed by the way Nicki, the victim in the case, didn't allow her victimhood to define her.

The following day, Donovan Ford was the first witness the prosecution called to testify. Patrick showed the jury harassing text messages Donovan received from Tim, and he played angry voicemails Tim left for Donovan once he learned his phone number.

When Patrick started asking Donovan about the false child abuse allegations that followed, the desperate nature of the defendant somehow shone through even further. Tim subjected Donovan to almost unthinkable harassment very early in Donovan's relationship with Nicki, but he stayed with her. Even as Nicki's ex tried to get Donovan fired and eventually tried to get him prosecuted for child abuse, Donovan never left Nicki.

Even when he temporarily moved back to Colorado to shield his own children from the chaos, he and Nicki never broke up. Donovan's commitment to her showed the jury that Nicki's testimony was credible beyond any doubt.

After thirteen more witnesses—bringing the grand total to forty-one—the prosecution rested its case. The trial had already stretched much longer than the jury was told it would last, with Judge Askalani giving them the entire week of Thanksgiving off. More than three weeks had passed since opening statements.

Now, it was the defense's turn. As they turned to Larry after a brief break, however, he surprised the members of the jury.

"The defense will not be calling any witnesses, your honor," Larry said.

"The defense rests?" Judge Askalani asked.

"That's right," Larry confirmed.

"Do you feel like you've had enough time to talk to Mr. Reed about your rights?" Judge Askalani asked Tim.

"Yes, ma'am. And, plus, I feel like I've testified twice already since I've been in here, so," Tim responded.

The jury did hear Tim repeat his same excuses over and over in the body camera videos and police interviews that were played as exhibits throughout the trial. Still, after Tim's attorney insinuated for weeks that he would play recordings that could prove Tim's innocence, the news that Tim wouldn't take the stand in his own defense landed with a thud—shocking the two prosecutors who had spent countless hours prepping for cross examination. Laura and the other jurors thought to themselves that it was probably for the best. The jury was ready to listen to closing arguments and finally begin deliberating without any witnesses offering testimony to shore up Tim's story.

CHAPTER THIRTY-EIGHT

In his closing argument to the jury, prosecutor Patrick Lofton acknowledged it might be obvious to them at that point that Colleen Larson was the shooter. He wanted to make sure they also had no doubt that Tim directed Colleen to do it.

"What would drive her to try to do this? She's not the one who's been in a four-year custody battle. She's not the one who had a judge tell her, 'You can't see your child unless there's a third party watching.' She's not the one who wrote 'Slut 4 Cops' on Nicole Lenway's garage. She's not the one who left crazy voicemails for Donovan Ford. That's all him," Patrick said.

Patrick reminded the jury how, on the night of the shooting, Sergeant Mark Suchta checked Tim's phone. The detective did not find a single call or text to or from Tim's live-in girlfriend, Colleen, on the night of the shooting. Not to let her know he'd be home late, not to let her know Nicki had been shot, not to let her know police needed to talk to him.

"He knows that communication with her during this time is going to look bad. It's going to suggest coordination. And so under these facts, the absence of that suggests coordination," Patrick said.

Patrick reminded jurors how video evidence debunked Tim's claim that he had Superman logos on his truck prior to the shooting and how incriminating Tim's attempted subterfuge looked, including his reporting his license plates stolen the day before the shooting. Patrick called it a plot that came at the end of ten years of hell that Tim caused Nicki—a plot that was put into motion after a judge ordered Tim's return to supervised visitation of his son.

"Imagine the anger that caused. Imagine the frustration. Think about that e-mail that Colleen Larson wrote. Think about how this was building in his head, and he felt like there was nothing else he could do, so he got his girlfriend to do this. It's really that simple."

The jury began deliberating at 3:15 p.m. on November 29, 2022, after hearing defense attorney Larry Reed's closing argument and Judge Shereen Askalani's instructions. After selecting a foreperson, the jury began going through the main points of the trial and asking what everyone in the room thought of them. Did anyone believe the black truck wasn't Tim's Dodge? Not a single person raised their hand. Did anyone think Colleen wasn't the shooter? No one raised their hand.

The jurors noted the evidence of technology that Tim wasn't able to outsmart. Being the only one with access to his surveillance camera log-in, it seemed clear that Tim deleted the two incriminating videos of Colleen leaving and returning in the truck. The Dodge Ram's location data, which Tim clearly hadn't accounted for, was impossible to explain away. Tim's entire defense sounded to the jurors like one enormous conspiracy theory. The sad fact was, Tim wasn't important enough for so many people to conspire against him. The jury knew that.

At 4:13 p.m., less than an hour after they received the case, the jurors held a vote among themselves for the less serious charge of aiding an offender after the fact. It was unanimous for guilty. They spent another seventeen minutes debating the aiding and abetting count, and then they told the bailiff they were ready to deliver their verdict. The difference in penalties between those two charges was enormous—likely thirty days in jail for aiding an offender after the fact and up to twenty years in prison for aiding and abetting first-degree attempted murder.

The short deliberation caught everyone in the case off guard. The attorneys and judge had discussed legal issues for several minutes after the jury left the courtroom, so the verdict actually came just fifty-six minutes after the court recessed. Judge Askalani had already told the attorneys they could go home, not expecting to have to call them back so quickly. A significant snowstorm had developed in Minneapolis that afternoon, and Larry let the court know it would take him a long time to get back to the courthouse.

Word that the jury was ready to read their verdict spread throughout the Minneapolis Police Department and the Hennepin County Attorney's Office. Available police officers headed to the courthouse as a show of support for Nicki, and other prosecutors filed into the courtroom, anxious for the result.

Nicki was in her vehicle after picking up Callahan from school when the victim advocate called to let her know the jury was ready. There was no way Nicki could make it home to drop off Cal and get back to the courthouse in time, so she and Donovan made a plan. They would both turn off their phones to avoid the inevitable flood of text messages. When they were home together and ready, they would turn on their phone and call the victim advocate to get the news.

When Nicki got home, she and Donovan went upstairs together, away from Cal and Donovan's kids. They called the victim advocate on speakerphone and waited.

"He's guilty on both counts."

Nicki felt disbelief at first. Then, sheer joy. She called her mom, who was out of state on a pre-planned vacation after attending the entire trial to that point for Nicki. Donovan and Nicki poured a glass of whiskey that evening, sitting together in their home with their kids, feeling for the first time that their lives really could be normal, calm, and without the chaos brought upon them by Tim. It simply felt like relief.

CHAPTER THIRTY-NINE

Nicki and Donovan attended Tim's sentencing hearing two months later, along with family, friends, and coworkers there in support. Tim had a small group of friends attending most of the trial, and that group was slightly larger to see Tim sentenced as well. Minnesota has sentencing guidelines passed by the legislature that limit the amount of discretion a judge has when weighing how much prison time they can hand down. The guideline range Judge Shereen Askalani could work with would give Tim anywhere between eight and a half to twelve years of actual time in prison, followed by a period of supervised release.

At sentencing hearings, victims are allowed to give an impact statement to tell the judge how the crime affected them and to provide input on what conditions they feel would be appropriate for the defendant's sentence.

Tim's eyes tracked Nicki and Donovan as Judge Askalani addressed her as "Mrs. Ford," and the married couple walked to the podium together.

"Every morning, I wake up, and I'm reminded by the visible scars on my body that mark the many violent and terrifying experiences that led me to fight for my life this last April. I can still feel the burning sensation and the utter fear of not being able to speak or to help myself. Time moved so fast and yet in slow motion. I truly thought I was dying that day and that I would never again get to see my loved ones. I am not only physically reminded of that day and all those before it in which I was victimized physically, mentally, emotionally, and financially, but I am left with the emotional scars and the persisting trauma from years of having to plead for my truth to be heard and seen," Nicki began in her victim impact statement.

Nicki wanted her statement to expose Tim for who he truly was. She aimed to show he was dangerous—not just in her opinion as an ex-girlfriend, but as a matter of objective fact—despite what the respected personas "Atlas" and "Master Amacher" projected to others. Nicki explained how Tim's accusations, even from behind bars—like his evidence-tampering claim—triggered further investigation and interrogation.

"Rather than taking responsibility, he continues to lie and project blame. I see him for what he is, and I hope others do, too. I wish I would have had the strength to confront him or to expose him for who he was long before today, but I have learned, through years of therapy, that this is exactly what he conditioned me to do. I always felt like I was the problem, like I deserved his anger, harsh words, deceit, and fury, undeserving of happiness and love. I have learned so much about myself, and I'm so glad that I at least had the courage to leave and want something better for myself and for my son," Nicki said.

Over the five years of false accusations after the custody battle began, Tim always claimed he was acting to protect his son. But Nicki had come to see the truth: Tim never truly wanted custody of Callahan—he wanted to punish her for leaving him. As Tim's control over Nicki slipped, he began to spiral. Like many abusers, he lashed out. But Tim took it further than anyone could have imagined.

"Your Honor, I want to thank you for the opportunity to be heard. After years of being silenced, shamed, and having to defend myself, it is encouraging to be able to speak freely without fear of retaliation or punishment. It has been over five years of threats and harassment, preceded by another five years of mental, physical, and emotional abuse. I have become aware of previous girlfriends and friends who all say Tim acted with a vengeance toward them as well when he felt he lost control or influence. The custody evaluator in family court gave him numerous opportunities to change, and he showed he was incapable of that. And given that he has shown no remorse for any of his actions, he is clearly capable and likely to do this again if the situation arises. The next time, his victim may not be as lucky," Nicki said.

Nicki addressed the selfishness of Tim's actions and how they affected Callahan. The cruelty, manipulation, coaching, and confusion to which Tim subjected their innocent son, all in the name of revenge, was unforgivable. Nicki asked Judge Askalani to give the maximum sentence.

"I fear for the day he's ultimately released. He will not stop. He is self-serving, and I know losing this battle will only fuel his rage further. I know someday, again, I will have to face his wrath. Please give me and my family the safety and security we deserve to heal from all the trauma," Nicki finished.

Since he chose not to testify in his own defense at the trial, a mix of anticipation and dread filled the courtroom as Judge Askalani gave Tim the opportunity to speak before handing down the sentence. He noticeably did not acknowledge Nicki as "Mrs. Ford," and he predictably began with complaints about what he called a broken justice system.

"Three weeks of a smear campaign, three weeks and over one hundred witnesses listed, witnesses that were nothing more than coworkers, colleagues, cohorts, and companions. Over one hundred witnesses listed, and not one person could say that they saw me do anything. Me and Mr. Reed, still to this day, question why I'm still sitting here. It's obvious that Ms. Lenway got shot. I'm not denying that. And I am empathetic that she had to go through that; however, no one to this day has seen or said that I've done anything," Tim said. "The prosecutor's office did display a show of smoke and mirrors, ending with an inference without any support or facts—simply relying just on the smear campaign. So, in other words: 'If we make him look like a bad guy, he must be a bad guy.'"

Tim then pivoted to a religious message, claiming no one but God could judge him. He cast police and prosecutors as Satan's servants masquerading as agents of righteousness. He described himself as a servant of Christ. As his allocution dragged on, Tim spoke of devotion and personal transformation through faith—a narrative sharply at odds with his actions exposed during the trial.

Judge Askalani's role during testimony was simply to make legal rulings and keep the case on track. At sentencing, she was finally allowed to share her own opinion before she ruled on Tim's fate. The judge noted that Tim had taken no accountability and shown no remorse.

"It appears that you have been promoting this false narrative about Mrs. Ford for so long that you may actually believe it at this time," Judge Askalani said.

In determining Tim's fate, Judge Askalani acknowledged a point Patrick had made during his argument. Callahan was now six years old. If she were to give Tim the maximum sentence allowed, that would ensure Tim would remain locked up until Cal was eighteen, helping ensure his safety and independence from his biological father. That is what Judge Askalani decided, handing down the maximum 216-month sentence, which would amount to twelve years in prison followed by five years of supervised release. Two deputies approached Tim and led him out of the courtroom and out of Nicki's life for the immediate future.

CHAPTER FORTY

Colleen decided not to take her case to trial after Tim's conviction, and her attorney let the court know she planned to plead guilty. Since her proffer interview did not result in any plea deal or trial testimony, Judge Shereen Askalani would be free to sentence Colleen to whatever she believed was fitting under Minnesota's sentencing guidelines.

After the proffer interview, Colleen's attorney, Dan Adkins, told the court that she was still stuck under Tim's influence after being groomed by the taekwondo master from as early as age twelve.

"He is her 'master,' but sadly, it is more than a double entendre as it speaks of his role in their relationship," Adkins wrote. "Ms. Larson has essentially spent half her life connected to and then ultimately subjected to Mr. Amacher's manipulation, control, and abuse."

With the passage of ten months since the shooting, the majority of that time with Colleen free on bail and attending counseling, prosecutors hoped Colleen would give a more detailed and accurate account of the attempted murder plot when she entered her guilty plea. At her plea hearing, however, Colleen shared minimal new information.

She acknowledged that Tim spoke about his desire to "remove Nicki from the equation" and essentially replace her with Colleen as "little man's mother." Colleen said it was Tim's idea for her to shoot Nicki and added that he removed the license plates from the Dodge Ram to avoid detection. But Colleen offered little more.

When prosecutor Patrick Lofton started questioning Colleen, she then walked back some of her admissions and suggested that Tim didn't know she was going to carry out the shooting that day.

"What'd he say to you about it?" Patrick asked.

"Nothing much, to be honest," Colleen answered.

"What was the 'nothing much?' What did he say?" Patrick asked.

"I really don't recall," Colleen answered.

Colleen went on to tell Patrick that she and Tim did not discuss the shooting at all in the week that followed before each of them was arrested. The prosecutor didn't believe it for a second. Judge Askalani wasn't satisfied either.

"I would like you to tell me in your own words why you're guilty of this offense," Judge Askalani said.

"Because I wanted to reunite Tim and his son," Colleen flatly stated.

The judge then walked Colleen through all the details leading up to the shooting again, including Tim telling Colleen what time Nicki would show up at FamilyWise to pick up Callahan.

"Why was he telling you that information?" Judge Askalani asked.

"Because he wanted me to kill Ms. Lenway," Colleen responded.

That was as good as they were going to get. Despite Colleen's attorney's best efforts to present his client as cooperative in the investigation, she simply wanted to plead guilty while blaming Tim as little as necessary.

At Colleen's sentencing hearing a month later, Patrick cautioned the judge not to assume Tim was a "sorcerer" who could achieve literal mind control of others. At the same time, attorney Dan Adkins, in arguing for a lighter sentence, continued to portray Colleen as an additional victim of an evil man.

"The manipulation, Your Honor, is so obvious, so clear. She was utterly overborne in this instance by that man," Dan said. "Tim Amacher destroyed her conscience, destroyed her capacity to be human."

When Nicki approached the podium to once again give a victim impact statement, however, she articulated Colleen's free will better than anyone in the courtroom: that the twenty-four-year-old shooter made a choice to try to end the life of someone she didn't even really know.

"I'm a stranger to her who happens to be the mother of the child she wanted to claim and an ex-girlfriend of a partner she wants a future with. She has admitted her intent and her eagerness to follow through with such violent and traumatizing actions on that fateful day. She stood over me, which felt like only inches away, continuing in her attempts to end my life, even pursuing me after I fled from her. She has even admitted she had every intention of killing me. She was less than forthcoming, uninformative, and unhelpful in the investigation, prolonging our pain and our little sense of justice we might be able to receive in knowing the truth, the entire truth," Nicki said.

Nicki revealed that she heard through mutual friends that while out on bail, Colleen had continued to have contact with Tim's inner circle. Colleen had communicated her love for him and continued hopes for a future with him, even nearly a year following the shooting. Nicki didn't see that as evidence of someone bettering herself and healing after escaping Tim's control.

Concerning Colleen's guilty plea, Nicki illustrated the difference between that and a show of remorse. Colleen was caught on camera, which left her little choice but to admit her actions. Nicki pointed out that Colleen insisted to police she was not manipulated.

Similar to the contradictions between Tim's words and actions, Nicki highlighted the sad irony of Colleen claiming she carried out the plot to try to help Callahan. As a result of Colleen's actions, Cal suffered trauma, fear, and heartbreak. Nicki described Colleen's blind devotion and infatuation with Tim as creating a delusional fantasy and skewed reality. And she said those clear red flags should be seen as future signs of danger as well.

"She's either easily coerced into taking a stranger's life based on a false reality and lies, or she truly wanted to. This is scary for us and scary for society as a whole," Nicki said. "I don't know what's worse—a vindictive ex who manipulates someone else to kill someone or a vulnerable stranger who blindly agrees to take someone's life without a second thought and zero remorse. Both are incredibly dangerous, both are equally culpable, and I think their sentencing should reflect that."

Judge Askalani was moved by Nicki's words and agreed with her viewpoint on Colleen's lack of remorse. The judge listened to Colleen's father speak about the Larson family's view on Tim's control and how Colleen changed and shut out friends once she was isolated with Tim. However, Colleen seemed only to be remorseful for the impact her actions had on her family and on her life, the judge noted. Colleen appeared to be unaffected by what she had done to Nicki and her loved ones. And it seemed to Judge Askalani that portraying Colleen as a brainwashed innocent was a stretch.

"By everyone's accounts, Ms. Larson has been described as naive, immature at times, and easily manipulated; however, she's also a twenty-five-year-old woman who is educated; she's a graduate from a university; she was a productive, functioning adult in society," Judge Askalani said.

She handed down a prison sentence just short of the maximum, 198 months, which would amount to eleven years locked up followed by five and a half years of supervised release. Colleen would spend nearly as much time in prison as Tim, a term that would have been exponentially less if only she had fully opened up about how she and Tim planned the attempted murder of Nicole Lenway.

CHAPTER FORTY-ONE

In early 2025, an honest conversation with his mother gave eight-year-old Callahan a deeper understanding of his family. For the first time, Nicki told Cal that his grandpa, Joe—who adopted Nicki and her twin sister Chantal after marrying their mother in 1995—wasn't technically "blood-related" to her. Nicki showed Cal how that never mattered; he had always been her dad. Cal immediately recognized the correlation to his relationship with his own father figure.

"Yeah, that's totally what it is. Donovan is my dad, and that's OK!" Callahan said.

Nicki believes she never felt the need to seek out her own biological father because Joe completely filled that void during her childhood. She never felt like anything was missing. Nicki and Donovan are providing the same environment in their home. She knows Cal will continue to have questions throughout his life, but she wants to ensure he never feels anything is lacking.

Callahan began calling Donovan "Dad" and gradually transitioned into calling his biological father "Tim" over the three years following the shooting. Through careful therapy sessions, professionals trained in the most challenging conversations helped the boy learn and understand what Tim had done to his mom. The Fords can see that Cal worries about Nicki and occasionally reflects on Tim's actions.

Donovan was raised to believe that a stepfather's role is to serve as a good role model without stepping on the biological father's toes. Even when Tim began his harassing calls, the only response Donovan ever sent was an agreement to meet during his lunch break in Minneapolis, believing that a conversation and an attempt to find mutual understanding would be necessary since he would be part of Nicki and Callahan's lives. After Tim tried to twist the terms of the meeting, Donovan had to let it go. His philosophy regarding his role in Callahan's life changed after everything Tim did to put himself in prison for the rest of Callahan's childhood. Donovan loves Callahan and treats him the same as his two older children.

Callahan gained those two siblings when Nicki married Donovan before the trial. Then, in November 2023, he welcomed a baby sister when Nicki gave birth to a little girl. Life has been normal for the Ford family since the criminal court case concluded in March 2022. For them, that is no small feat. Nicki's best friend, Anya Esch, senses Nicki is able to relax for the first time in ten years. Their family get-togethers no longer include sharing details of the latest false claim and strategizing how Nicki should deal with Tim. She finally seems to be at peace.

Donovan sees daily how the removal of that perpetual stress and anxiety has helped Nicki thrive. Yet, the Ford family knows a clock is ticking. Tim's release from prison is scheduled for

April 2034. They only hope that by then, Tim has found a way to move past his rage and vengeance. They hope he finds a way to move on with his life and leave them alone.

Nicki had long believed Tim was capable of murder. She knew that, eventually, something like the shooting would have to happen for him to finally be stopped—only then could she and Cal find reprieve. They say a mother would do anything for her child. Although she wishes it could have happened differently, Nicki took two bullets. And because of that sacrifice, Callahan will grow up free from the chaos and mayhem Tim "Atlas" Amacher inflicted upon them. They survived him, and now they get to live.

ABOUT THE AUTHOR

Lou Raguse is a journalist specializing in crime and courts. Since 2005, he has reported for NBC, CBS, and FOX affiliates in Minnesota, New York, Arizona, and South Dakota.

His first book, *Vanished in Vermillion*, uncovered new information in a fifty-year-old cold case and was selected as the 2025 One Book Siouxland honor.

He has received numerous regional Emmy Awards for his reporting and an Edward R. Murrow Award for his podcast, *88 Days: The Jayme Closs Story*, which reached the top ten on iTunes.

Raguse lives in Minnesota with his wife and two children and spends much of his free time coaching their youth sports teams.

You can follow Raguse's latest by subscribing to his free newsletter here: https://thenewsman.substack.com/.